FlyHigh 4 — Contents

① Where's Toto?

1 Write the names. Then choose and write.

~~Dr Wild~~   Oscar   Jack   Kelly   Toto   ~~toucan~~   niece   nephew   detective

Dr Wild

1 Toto is a ___toucan___ .

2 Dr Wild is an animal _____ .

3 Jack is Dr Wild's _____ .

4 Kelly is Dr Wild's _____ .

2 Choose, write and match.

clever   ~~lazy~~   helpful   friendly

a ___He's lazy.___   **b** _____   **c** _____   **d** _____

I got 10 out of 10 in my English test. __c__

Can I clean the board, please? _____

I don't want to go to school. _____

Hello! You look great today. _____

3 Write the questions and answers.

1 __Is__ Dr Wild an Animal Detective? Yes, she is.

2 _____ she work in the zoo? _____

3 _____ Oscar friendly? _____

4 _____ he like Kelly and Jack? _____

5 _____ Kelly and Jack like cats? _____

6 _____ they like Oscar? _____

④ Choose and write.

~~stay/stays~~   help/helps   play/plays   eat/eats   drink/drinks   work/works   find/finds

Jack and Kelly **(1)** ....stay............... with their aunt every summer.

Dr Wild **(2)** .... at home.

She **(3)** .... missing animals.

Jack and Kelly **(4)** .... their aunt with her work.

They **(5)** .... with Oscar, too.

Oscar **(6)** .... a lot of fish and he **(7)** .... milk every day.

⑤ Write. Use **don't** or **doesn't**.

1 Jack and Kelly stay with their grandma every summer.
...No, they don't stay with their grandma every summer.

2 Dr Wild works in a zoo.
....

3 Dr Wild finds missing cars.
....

4 The children do their homework with Oscar.
....

5 Oscar eats lots of salad.
....

6 Oscar drinks orange juice every day.
....

⑥ Circle and answer about you.

1 Do / Are you like books? ....
2 Do / Are you friendly? ....
3 Do / Are you lazy? ....

4 Do / Are you think you're helpful? ....
5 Do / Are you play a sport every day? ....

2 We're getting ready!

1 Label the picture.

can opener   compass   binoculars   passport   torch   ~~diary~~   laptop

1 .....diary......

2 Look at Exercise 1 and write.

1 Dr Wild is packing passports and a ....

2 Jack ....

3 Oscar ....

4 Kelly ....

3 Circle, choose and write.

swimsuits   ball   sun cream   water   boots   ~~shampoo~~   oranges   tomato   cheese   peaches   bread

1 I'm washing my hair. I need / needs ...shampoo............ and ....

2 My brother is playing football. He need / needs a .... and some ....

3 We're making some juice. We need / needs .... and ....

4 Mum is making a sandwich. She need / needs .... , ... and a ....

5 My friends are going to the beach. They need / needs .... and ....

④ **Look and write the names.**

1 They're wearing shorts, they're playing and they're laughing. _Gemma and Penny_

2 They're cooking and singing. ....

3 He's wearing shorts and he's drinking. ....

4 She's wearing jeans and she's sleeping. ....

5 He's reading and eating. ....

⑤ **Look at Exercise 4 and write.**

1 What's Katy doing? _She's sleeping._

2 Is Jim drinking? ....

3 Is Gemma wearing a skirt? ....

4 Are they laughing? ....

5 What's Ken wearing? ....

6 What are Ken and Mary cooking? ....
....

7 What's Jim eating? ....

8 Are Penny and Gemma drinking? ....

⑥ **Now correct the sentences.**

1 Tom is drinking milk.   _Tom is drinking water._

2 Katy is wearing a sweater. ....

3 Mary and Ken are eating burgers. ....

4 Jim is writing a book. ....

3 Dr Wild drives well.

1 Do the crossword. Write the adverbs. Then complete the sentence below.

Do this crossword .... !

2 Choose and write.

1 bad/badly   Look at that man! He's driving very *badly* ....
2 quick/quickly   I'm doing my homework ....
3 careful/carefully   The children are crossing the road ....
4 happy/happily   My cat has got some fish and she's ....
5 good/well   My teacher speaks English very ....
6 quiet/quietly   Please be .... !
7 slow/slowly   My grandma is tired and she's walking home ....

3 Match and complete.

happily   slowly   ~~quickly~~   quietly

1 It's raining!   a She's playing ....
2 My dad's car is very old.   b Let's run home *quickly* ....
3 Ssh! The baby is sleeping.   c He drives ....
4 My little sister loves her new ball.   d Talk ....

8

④ **Look, circle and complete. Choose words from Exercise 1.**

1 The monkeys is / are eating ...quickly........... .
2 The acrobat is / are walking ....
3 The girls is / are laughing ....
4 The dancer is / are dancing ....

5 The clown is / are dancing ....
6 The boy is / are speaking ....
7 The horses is / are running ....

⑤ **Read and complete the chart.**

eat my breakfast	do my homework	tidy my bedroom	play football
quickly			

Hi, I'm Jake. I don't eat my breakfast slowly. I eat it quickly.
I don't want to be late for school! I don't do my homework quickly.
I do it carefully. I don't want to make mistakes. I tidy my bedroom
slowly. It isn't fun! I love football. I play football well!

⑥ **Write sentences about you.**

1 happily I play with my friends happily.
2 carefully ....
3 slowly ....

4 quickly ....
5 badly ....
6 well ....

Let's phone Mel.

SKILLS 4

Writing Class: punctuation

① Write these sentences. Add the punctuation.

1 my name is kit baker .....My name is Kit Baker. ....

2 im 11 years old and I live in bristol ....

3 im not very tall and ive got short brown hair ....

4 ive got a big family my mum my dad two brothers and one sister ....

....

5 what do you do at the weekends ....

---

② Match. Then complete the answers about you.

1 What's your name?

2 How old are you?

3 What do you look like?

4 Where do you live?

5 What's your family like?

6 What do you do at the weekends?

7 What do you think you do well?

a At the weekend I like ....

b I think I .... well .

c I've got a .... family, my ....

d I live in ....

e I'm .... old .

f My name is ....

g I'm .... and I've got .... eyes and .... hair .

③ Write a composition about you.

Write about:
- what you look like.
- your family.
- what you do at the weekends.

All about me!

_____

_____

_____

_____

_____

_____

_____

_____

④ Circle the correct answer.

1 eight, nine, double one, oh, three   **a** 890113   **(b)** 891103

2 six, double five, seven, double two   **a** 655722   **b** 677522

3 oh, three, oh, nine, four, one   **a** 030941   **b** 033940

4 double eight, five, four, three, oh   **a** 855430   **b** 885430

⑤ Write the numbers.

1 oh, five, seven, double six, two   ....

2 four, double one, oh, three, six   ....

3 double seven, nine, two, oh, one   ....

⑥ Read and match.

1 Let's phone   **a** number?

2 What's her phone   **b** you doing?

3 Where   **c** Beth.

4 What are   **d** soon!

5 Do you want to   **e** come to my house later?

6 See you   **f** are you?

⑦ Look and write Danny's questions.

Danny

Max

Danny: Hi, **(1)** ___Max._____

Max: Hello, Danny.

Danny: **(2)** ....

Max: I'm in town.

Danny: **(3)** ....

Max: I'm buying a T-shirt.

Danny: **(4)** .... a pizza later?

Max: Yes, great!

Danny: OK, see you soon.

Max: Bye!

FlyHigh File: Countries and nationalities

1 **Choose and label the pictures.**

~~nationality~~   country   language   flag   capital city

1 .....nationality.....

2 ....

3 ....

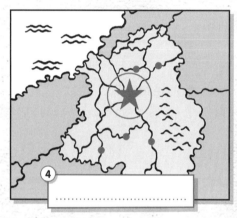

4 ....

5 ....

2 **Look at your Pupil's Book, page 15. Complete the chart.**

Country	(1)	(2)	Nationality	Flag
Turkey	Ankara	Turkish	Turkish	red and white
(3)	Warsaw	(4)	(5)	(6) ....
Ukraine	(7)	(8)	(9)	(10) ....
Romania	Bucharest	Romanian	Romanian	blue, yellow and red
(11)	(12)	Spanish	Argentinian	(13) ....
Bulgaria	Sofia	Bulgarian	Bulgarian	white, green and red
(14)	(15)	Russian	(16)	(17) ....
Hungary	Budapest	Hungarian	Hungarian	red, white and green

12

③ **Look, read and write.**

I'm Amy and I'm from England.
I live in London.
England is in the United Kingdom.

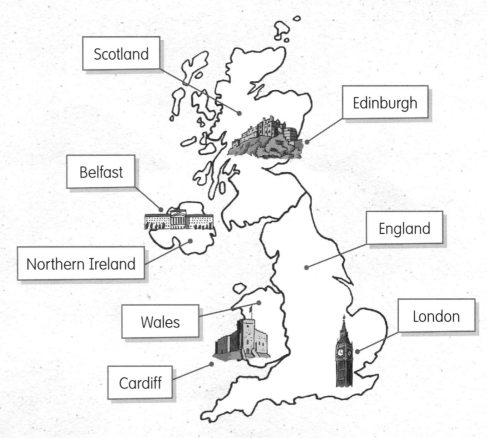

Scotland

Edinburgh

Belfast

Northern Ireland

Wales

Cardiff

England

London

There are three other countries in the UK:

(1) .... , **(2)** .... and **(3)** .... **(4)** ....
is the capital of England and the UK. **(5)** .... is the capital of Scotland,
(6) .... is the capital of Wales and **(7)** .... is the capital of
Northern Ireland. The flag of the United Kingdom has a name. It's called the Union Jack.
It's **(8)** .... , **(9)** .... and **(10)** ....
I'm **(11)** .... and I speak **(12)** ....

④ **Draw your flag. Then complete the text about you.**

My name is ....
and I'm from ....

My nationality is ....
The capital city of my country is

....

and the colours of our flag are

....

The language I speak is ....

5 There was a storm.

① Circle the odd one out.

1	car	⟨in⟩	boat	train
2	worried	tired	bored	next
3	morning	front	night	evening
4	behind	storm	thunder	lightning

② Write the circled words in Exercise 1 and match.

1 The cat is
...in... the boat. [c]

2 The cat is
.... to the boat. [ ]

3 The cat is in
.... of the boat. [ ]

4 The cat is
.... the boat. [ ]

 a
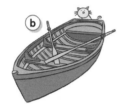 b
 c
 d

③ Complete the chart and write.

Noun	Adjective
cloud	cloudy
rain	
	snowy
	stormy
sun	
wind	

1 There was a lot of ...snow... .

2 It was ....

3 There was a big black .... in the sky.

4 It was ....

5 It was ....

6 There was a .... with thunder and lightning.

4 **Write was, wasn't, were or weren't.**

Yesterday Claudia and Magnus
(1) ...... _were_ ...... on a boat. Toto
(2) .... on the boat, too. In the
night there **(3)** .... a terrible storm
with thunder and lightning. There
(4) .... a lot of heavy rain but
Claudia and Magnus **(5)** ....
worried – the boat **(6)** .... big
and they **(7)** .... inside in a warm
room. Only Toto **(8)** .... outside all
night. In the morning his feathers **(9)** ....
very wet. He **(10)** .... happy.

5 **Look, circle and answer.**

1 (Was)/ Were there a boat? ..... Yes, there was. .....

2 Was / Were there any birds? ....

3 Was / Were there any clouds? ....

4 Was / Were there any rain? ....

5 Was / Were there any children in the lake?

....

6 Was / Were there a fisherman in the boat?

6 **What about you? Write about yesterday. Use was, wasn't, were or weren't.**

1 It/cold and rainy. The weather/good. ....

2 There/a storm yesterday evening. It/a bad night. ....

3 My friends and I/at school. It/a holiday. ....

4 My mum and dad/at home in the evening. They/out. ....

5 Yesterday/a busy day. There/a lot to do. ....

6 We landed on a beach.

1 **Look and write the numbers.**

1   2   3   4   5   6

1	aquarium		pet shop		police station
	town hall		museum		café

2 **Read and write the places in Exercise 1.**

aquarium   town hall   café   ~~police station~~   museum   pet shop

1 In the ..police station.. , we asked the police officer for help.

2 We looked at the dinosaurs in the ....

3 We talked to the mayor in the ....

4 At the .... , we watched the fish.

5 We played with the rabbits in the ....

6 There were a lot of different cakes in the ....

3 **Look, read and match.**

①  ②  ③  ④

1 Yesterday morning	they helped	dinosaurs	in the museum.
2 Yesterday afternoon	they looked	on the swings	at home.
3 Yesterday evening	they painted	at the stars	in the park.
4 Last night	they played	their mum	in the sky.

4 Write the past tense forms.

In the park yesterday ….

1 The boy .... _listened_ .... (listen) to his music.
2 The man .... (walk) his dog.
3 The men .... (paint) the fence.
4 The girl .... (skip) happily.
5 The children .... (play) with a ball.
6 The women .... (talk).
7 The boy .... (look) at the birds.
8 The cat .... (jump) on the wall.

5 Read, write and match.

1 Yesterday afternoon Kelly and Jack .... _walked_ .... (walk) — the museum.
2 In the library they .... (look) — to the library.
3 Then they .... (visit) TV.
4 They .... (ask) at the books.
5 Then they .... (play) about the dinosaurs.
6 In the evening they .... (watch) with Oscar.

6 Look and write.

clean   drop   ~~paint~~   jump

At the beach yesterday...

1   She painted a picture.

2 ....

3 ....

4 ....

7 Did you talk to them?

1 Look, choose and write.

nose   moustache   face   beard   ~~blond~~   thin

This is Fred. He's got wavy **(1)** .....blond.........
hair. He's got a small **(2)** ....
and a **(3)** .... mouth.
He's got a **(4)** ....
but he hasn't got a **(5)** ....
He's got a friendly **(6)** ....

2 Look at Exercise 1 and answer.

What does Fred look like?

1 What's his hair like? ......It's wavy and blond.....

2 Does he have a moustache? ....

3 Does he have a beard? ....

4 Does he wear glasses? ....

5 Does he have a friendly smile? ....

3 Look, read and complete the chart.

Name	Jess		
Nationality			
Personality		friendly	

1 The person with a thin face was Jess.

2 The person with a big smile was friendly.

3 The person with a diary was French.

4 The person with binoculars was English.

5 The person with a moustache and beard was Ollie.

6 The person wearing glasses was helpful.

7 The person with wavy blond hair was Lucy.

8 The person with a small nose was kind.

9 The person with a torch was Russian.

4 Write the opposite sentences.

1 Kelly showed the boy a photo of Toto.   _Kelly didn't show the boy a photo of Toto._

2 A car stopped near Kelly in the morning.   ....

3 The boy noticed a cat in the car.   ....

4 The boy looked at Magnus's face.   ....

5 The boy didn't talk to Kelly and Jack.   ....

6 They followed the boy.   ....

5 Read and write the past tense forms.

Yesterday morning Paul **(1)** ...._walked_.......... (walk) to the park where he

(2) .... (wait) for his friend, Jess. They **(3)** ....

(climb) a tree and then they **(4)** .... (argue).

Jess **(5)** .... (want) to play with some other children but Paul

(6) .... (not do). Jess and the children **(7)** ....

(play) football. Paul **(8)** .... (stay) and **(9)** ....

(watch) them for ten minutes, then he **(10)** .... (walk) home.

On the way, he **(11)** .... (talk) to a boy and a girl.

They **(12)** .... (ask) him some questions about a car and a toucan.

6 Read Exercise 5 again and answer.

1 Did Jess wait for Paul in the park?   ...._No, she didn't._................

2 Did Jess and Paul climb a tree in the park?   ....

3 Did Jess want to play with the other children?   ....

4 Did Jess and Paul both play football?   ....

5 Did Paul talk to a boy and a girl on the way home?   ....

6 Did he ask them about a toucan?   ....

7 Now write questions and answers about yesterday.

1 Paul/walk to the park   _Did Paul walk to the park yesterday?_   _Yes, he did._

2 Jess and Paul/argue   ....

3 Paul/play with the other children   ....

4 the boy and girl/ ask questions about Jess   ....

8 SKILLS — I'd like tickets for the museum, please.

Writing Class: and, but ✏️

① Write and or but.

1 In the morning I cleaned my bedroom ....*and*........ helped my mum.

2 After lunch I walked to the pet shop .... it wasn't open.

3 In the evening I stayed at home .... watched a film.

4 I liked the film .... it wasn't funny.

② Rewrite the sentences with and or but.

1 Today was cloudy. It wasn't cold. ...Today was cloudy but it wasn't cold....

2 In the morning I played tennis with my friend. I didn't play well.

....

3 In the afternoon my dad and I visited the aquarium. We visited the café.

....

4 I liked the dolphins. I didn't like the octopus.

....

5 Then we walked to the bus stop. We waited for a bus.

....

6 At home my dad cooked some pasta. I helped him.

....

③ Write your diary for last Saturday.

Write:

- what the weather was like.
- two things you did in the morning.
- one thing you did and one thing you didn't do in the afternoon.
- two things you did in the evening.

Saturday

In the morning ....

....

In the afternoon ....

....

In the evening ....

....

4 Number Danny's dialogue in the correct order.

☐ Yes, I'd like tickets for the museum, please.

1 Can I help you?

☐ The museum. Certainly. How many would you like?

☐ Two tickets, please. One adult and one child.

☐ Thank you.

☐ That's twelve euros.

5 Choose and complete Max's dialogue.

please   I'd like   tickets   ~~help~~   How many   Thank you

Ticket seller: Can I **(1)** ....help.... you?

Max: Yes, **(2)** .... tickets for the cinema, **(3)** ....

Ticket seller: The cinema. Certainly. **(4)** .... would you like?

Max: Four **(5)** ...., please. Four children.

Ticket seller: That's sixteen euros.

Max: **(6)** ....

6 Read the dialogues in Exercises 4 and 5. Look and write Max, Danny or X.

1 ....Max............   ....X............   ....Danny............

2 ....

3 ....

FlyHigh File: Hurricanes

① Choose and label the pictures.

hurricane   flood   tornado   ~~natural disaster~~

a ....

b ....

c ....

d natural disaster

② Read and circle.

1 Storms (produce) / rain about 1,000 tornadoes in the USA every year.

2 Tornadoes usually watch / last about four or five minutes.

3 More than 80 people die / wash in tornadoes every year.

4 Tornado winds can travel / stay more than 400 kilometres an hour.

5 Tornadoes can come / destroy houses and trees.

③ Read, choose and write.

died   destroyed   travelled   floods   lasted   ~~hurricane~~

I remember a terrible **(1)** __hurricane__ when I was ten years old. It **(2)** .... from

Cuba to the USA. On August 17 1969 I watched it on TV. It was my tenth birthday.

The name of the hurricane was Hurricane Camille. It **(3)** .... nine days.

The winds destroyed many houses, trees and cars and there were terrible **(4)** ....

Two hundred and fifty-six people **(5)** .... We do not know how fast the winds were

because the hurricane **(6)** .... the weather instruments.

④ Read and tick the things you need when a hurricane comes.

HELP! IT'S A HURRICANE

Are you ready? Do you know what to do when a hurricane comes? It's summer and it's the hurricane season here in the USA. Do you live in the east of the country? This is the hurricane zone and you must plan what to do before a hurricane comes. You must choose a safe room in the house and have a bag ready. In the bag, you need clothes, money, a mobile phone, a torch and a radio. You must also have food and water for a week. Do you have family or friends in other cities? Sometimes you must phone your friend and move to another town to be safe. You must think what to do about your pets when you go.

⑤ Read and circle.

1 The hurricane season is in the		spring.	⊙summer.⊙	winter.
2 People must		watch the ocean.	have a dog.	make plans.
3 At home, people must look for		a big map.	a safe room.	good boots.
4 They need enough to eat and drink for a		week.	month.	year.
5 Sometimes people must go to another		bed.	town.	country.
6 When people go to another place, they must think what to do with their		car.	camera.	pets.

⑥ Read and complete the chart.

4 – 8 July

On Monday the weather was lovely. It was hot and sunny. On Tuesday it was cloudy but it didn't rain. On Wednesday there was heavy rain all day. The rain stayed all Thursday and there was a storm with thunder and lightning in the evening. The rain stopped on Friday but it was cold and there were strong winds coming from the north.

Day	Weather	Day	Weather
Monday	☀		

The Fly High Review

1 Read, draw and colour.

 (a)

 (b)

 (c)

 (d)

1 She's got short brown wavy hair. She wears glasses.

2 He's got short black hair, a black moustache and a grey beard.

3 He's got short blond hair. He wears glasses.

4 She's got long wavy red hair.

2 Look and write questions and answers.

 (1) PETS

 (2) CINEMA

 (3) AQUARIUM

 (4) MUSEUM

1 café — Is she going to a café? — No, she isn't. She's going to a pet shop.

sunny — Is it sunny? — No, it isn't. It's cloudy.

2 town hall .... — ....

rainy .... — ....

3 park .... — ....

snowy .... — ....

4 police station .... — ....

windy .... — ....

3 Put the letters in the correct order and write.

1 (zyal) He's __lazy__ . He gets up very late.

2 (redylnif) She's .... She's talking to the new girl in the class.

3 (pleuhlf) They're .... They're cleaning the board for the teacher.

4 (eevlrc) She's .... She gets good marks for her homework.

④ Look and write.

a Yesterday

b Today

1 There were three passports.   There's one passport.

2 ....

3 ....

⑤ Look, write questions and answers.

a Amy John

John and Amy's day yesterday

b

1 they/walk/park ✓   Did they walk to the park yesterday? Yes, they did.

2 John/play/tennis ✗   Did John play tennis? No, he didn't. He

3 Amy/climb/mountain ✗

4 dog/jump/pool ✓

5 they/listen/band ✓

My English

How did I do? Write OK/Well/Very Well.

1 **Learn with Oscar**   I read/I'm reading/He eats quickly/I walked/Did they walk? ....

2 **New words**   niece/laptop/badly/passport/storm/aquarium/moustache/flood ....

3 **Writing**   Composition ....   Diary ....

4 **Conversations**   Making a phone call ....   Buying tickets ....

5 **Projects**   Drawing a flag ....   Writing a weather diary ....

Robinson Crusoe

1 **Do the crossword.**

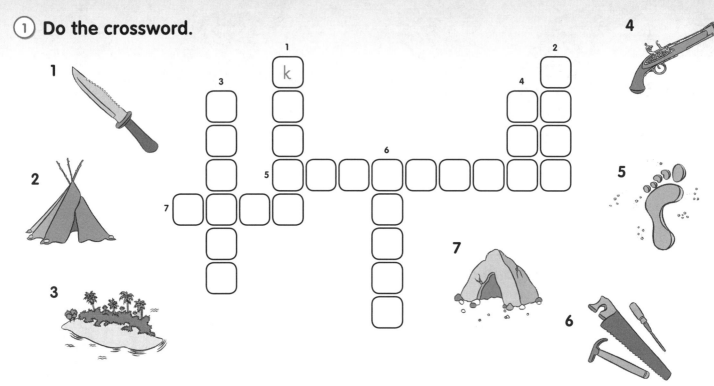

2 **Read Robinson Crusoe on pages 28–29 of your Pupil's Book.**
Number the pictures in order.

(3) **Look at Exercise 2, choose and write.**

a He makes a boat and gets tools, food and clothes from the ship.
b It rains a lot and Robinson Crusoe is sad.
c He makes a tent in a cave.
d ~~Robinson Crusoe leaves Brazil with ten other men.~~
e There's a great storm at sea.
f He sees a man's footprint on the beach.
g He doesn't know where he is. He hasn't got anything.
h He swims to the ship.

Picture One: ......Robinson Crusoe leaves Brazil with ten other men.........

Picture Two: ....

Picture Three: ....

Picture Four: ....

Picture Five: ....

Picture Six: ....

Picture Seven: ....

Picture Eight: ....

(4) **Write True or False.**

1 Robinson Crusoe wanted to go to the island. ......False............

2 Ten men are lost in the sea. ....

3 Crusoe gets tools, food and water from the ship. ....

4 The weather is always sunny on the island. ....

5 He's sad in September because it's his birthday. ....

6 He knows who made the footprint on the beach. ....

(5) **Match the sentences with the same meaning.**

1 I've got nothing with me.   **a** I'm not well.

2 It leaves me on the beach.   **b** The weather is stormy.

3 I am very tired and ill.   **c** The sea takes me to an island.

4 I make eleven journeys between the   **d** I haven't got any food, clothes or tools.
   beach and the ship.

5 The wind and rain are strong all night.   **e** I go to the ship lots of times in a small boat.

9 Magnus and Claudia had an accident!

① Choose and write.

farm   grass   horse   pond   owl   ~~bull~~   cow

1 This animal is big and black.   bull
2 You can ride this animal.   ....
3 Cows eat this. It's green.   ....
4 We get milk from this animal.   ....
5 Ducks sometimes swim here.   ....
6 Animals live here and farmers work here.   ....
7 This is a bird with big eyes. It flies at night.   ....

② Write every day or yesterday.

1 I go to school ...every day........ . I went to school ...yesterday........ .
2 I saw my friends .... I see my friends ....
3 My little brother is two years old. He falls over .... He fell over ....
4 I hear birds singing .... I heard birds singing ....
5 I had lots of homework .... I have lots of homework ....
6 My mum drove to work .... My mum drives to work ....

③ Read and circle.

I went to a farm yesterday with my family. We **(1)** see / saw some cows, horses and a bull. My dad **(2)** drove / drives the farmer's car. It was very old and he drove very **(3)** slow / slowly! There were lots of ducks in a **(4)** pond / farm. I heard a big splash. My brother fell in the pond! He **(5)** was / wasn't very happy but we had a great day.

4 Write. Then choose and complete the chart.

to school   some music on the radio   a funny film on TV   in the river   to the park
spaghetti for lunch   a good song   a white cat in the garden   ~~a Maths test~~   off my bike

have/ had	fall/	go/	see/	hear/
a Maths test				

5 Choose and write.

My brother had a party   ~~We went to a museum~~   We heard a bird

I saw my grandma   My dad fell off a horse

1 ...We went to a museum............... yesterday. It was very interesting.

2 .... on Saturday. It was his birthday.

3 .... last night. It was an owl.

4 .... yesterday. He wasn't happy.

5 .... last weekend. She was very well.

6 Choose and write the past tense forms.

go   ~~drive~~   hear   see   have   fall

1 My teacher ...drove............ her new car to school yesterday.

2 My friend .... in the river yesterday. He was wet!

3 We .... an English test at school yesterday.

4 I .... some lovely music on the radio yesterday.

5 My sister .... to school by bike yesterday.

6 I've got binoculars and yesterday I .... some beautiful birds.

7 What about you? Write true sentences.

1 This morning I ...had......... (have) .... for breakfast.

2 Last night I .... (hear) ....

3 Yesterday I .... (see) ....

4 Last weekend my dad .... (drive) ....

5 Last summer my family .... (go) ....

6 When I was young, I .... (fall) ....

10 Did they find Toto?

① Choose and write.

unhappy   confused   scared   ~~nervous~~

1 Lots of people are watching me. I can't sing. I'm very ___nervous.___

2 I don't know the answer to this question. Is it yes or no? I'm _____ .

3 My sister is _____ of big dogs.

4 The little girl is crying. She can't find her cat and she's _____ .

② Look and circle the correct answer.

①  ②  ③ ④

1 Did they have bread and honey for breakfast?   **a** Yes, they did.   **b** No, they didn't.

2 Did they ride their bikes to school?   **a** Yes, they did.   **b** No, they didn't.

3 Did she go home after school?   **a** Yes, she did.   **b** No, she didn't.

4 Did she swim in a river?   **a** Yes, she did.   **b** No, she didn't.

③ Write the questions in the correct order.

Claudia: **(1)** ___Did you see the tree?___   Did / see / tree ? / you / the

Magnus: No, I didn't.

Claudia: **(2)** _____   the / see / Did / pond ? / you

Magnus: No, I didn't.

Magnus: **(3)** _____   the / fall / Did / pond ? / you / in

Claudia: Yes, I did!

Magnus: **(4)** _____   wet ? / you / Did / get

Claudia: Yes, I did!

4 Read about Jimmy's day. Number the sentences in the correct order.

a [1] My name's Jimmy. I didn't have a good day yesterday!
I didn't wake up at seven o'clock. I didn't hear my alarm clock!

b [ ] I had lots of homework in the evening. I didn't know how to do my English homework.
I was confused! I was happy when it was time for bed!

c [ ] It rained and we didn't go out to play. I looked in my bag but I didn't have my lunch box.
I was hungry. My friend had two sandwiches but they fell on the floor.

d [ ] My mum didn't drive me to school. I ran but I was late for school and my teacher
was unhappy.

e [ ] We had a Maths test in the morning and I was nervous. I didn't know three of the answers.
I didn't do those questions.

5 Read Exercise 4 again. Answer the questions.

1 Did Jimmy hear his alarm clock at seven?   No, he didn't.

2 Did he go to school by car?   ....

3 Did he have a Maths test?   ....

4 Did he answer all the questions?   ....

5 Did he have a sandwich for lunch?   ....

6 Did he have homework in the evening?   ....

6 What about you? Write true sentences about your day yesterday.

1 see my teacher
   I saw my teacher./I didn't see my teacher.

2 hear my alarm clock in the morning
   ....

3 see my best friend
   ....

4 go to school by bus
   ....

5 have sandwiches for lunch
   ....

6 have lots of homework
   ....

11 Claudia couldn't hear.

1 Look, choose and write.

well   stomachache   cold   ~~headache~~   sore throat   earache

1 ....headache............

2 ....

3 ....

4 ....

5 ....

6 ....

2 Write and circle. Use words from Exercise 1.

1 She had a ...headache........... yesterday and she could /(couldn't) do her homework.

2 He had a .... yesterday and he could / couldn't go to school.

3 She was .... yesterday and she could / couldn't ride her bike.

4 He had a .... yesterday and he could / couldn't eat his breakfast.

5 She had an .... yesterday but she could / couldn't do a puzzle.

6 He had a .... yesterday and he could / couldn't sing.

3 Read and write.

Billy had a stomachache yesterday. What could he do? What couldn't he do?

go to school ✗	eat his dinner ✗	watch TV ✔
read books ✔	play football ✗	phone his friends ✔

1 ...He couldn't go to school...............................

2 ....

3 ....

4 ....

5 ....

6 ....

4 Write the opposite sentences.

1 It was stormy. He couldn't go out in his boat.   It wasn't stormy. He could go out in his boat.

2 It wasn't windy. We couldn't fly our kite.   ....

3 It was rainy. They couldn't play in the garden.   ....

4 It was sunny. She could wash her car.   ....

5 It was snowy. They could make a snowman.   ....

5 Read and circle.

1 I can / could speak English now.

2 I couldn't / can't speak English when I was a baby.

3 I had a headache yesterday and I can't / couldn't do my homework.

4 I think my friends are hiding. I can't / couldn't see them.

5 My mum made five sandwiches for me yesterday. I can't / couldn't eat them all.

6 I can / could walk when I was two but I can't / couldn't ride a bike.

6 Look, match and write.

This is Jack when he was four years old.

1 ride a bike   He couldn't ride a bike.   `d`

2 throw a ball   ....   ☐

3 read   ....   ☐

4 swim   ....   ☐

5 talk   ....   ☐

6 make a cake   ....   ☐

....

12 SKILLS I'm sorry I couldn't come.

Writing Class: *on, in, at,* with days and times ✎

① **Choose and complete.**

on	in	at
Monday		

half past eleven   ~~Monday~~   the evening   Wednesday   twelve o'clock   Saturday
the morning   the afternoon   eight o'clock

② **Write in, on or at.**

(1) ....On.... Monday I went to school **(2)** .... eight o'clock **(3)** .... the morning.
I had a swimming lesson **(4)** .... half past four **(5)** .... the afternoon
(6) .... Tuesday. I phoned my grandma **(7)** .... seven o'clock **(8)** ....
the evening **(9)** .... Sunday.

③ **Write a letter about last weekend.**

Write:
• where you went.
• when you went.
• who you went with.
• one thing you could see.
• one thing you couldn't do.

Dear .... ,
....
....
....
....
....
....
....
With love from ....

4 Read and match.

1 I was   **a** a headache.

2 I had   **b** ill.

3 Are you   **c** happened?

4 Did you   **d** all right now?

5 What   **e** have a good time?

5 Number the dialogue in the correct order.

a ☐ Yes, thank you. Did you have a good time?

b ☐ I was ill. I had a headache.

c ☐ Yes, it was great.

d ☐ Are you all right now?

e 1 I'm sorry I couldn't come to your party.

f ☐ That's OK. What happened?

6 Look and write.

Annie: (1) I'm sorry I couldn't come to the cinema.

Sam: That's OK. What happened?

Annie: (2) ....

Sam: Are you all right now?

Annie: Yes, thank you. Did you have a good time?

Sam: Yes, it was great.

Clare: (1) ....

Ben: That's OK. What happened?

Clare: (2) ....

Ben: Are you all right now?

Clare: Yes, thank you. Did you have a good time?

Ben: Yes, it was great.

FlyHigh File: Dinosaurs

1 Choose and write.

land   plants   lizards   ~~hunt~~

1   This is when an animal looks for other animals to eat.   ...hunt...

2   We live on this. It isn't the sky and it isn't the sea.   ....

3   These are small animals with four legs and long tails.   ....

4   These are green and you find them in the garden.   ....

2 Look, choose and write.

walked   ~~dinosaur~~   plants   legs   didn't   neck   was   couldn't   eat   long   had   lizards   could

The Brachiosaurus was a huge **(1)** ...dinosaur... . It had four **(2)** .... and a long **(3)** .... and tail and it **(4)** .... very heavy. It **(5)** .... very slowly and it **(6)** .... run. It ate **(7)** .... and leaves. It **(8)** .... hunt animals.

The Struthiomimus **(9)** .... two thin legs and a **(10)** .... neck and it **(11)** .... run very quickly. It didn't **(12)** .... plants. It ate insects and **(13)** ....

3 Read Exercise 2 and answer the questions.

1   Could the Brachiosaurus walk quickly?   No, it couldn't.

2   Could it run?   ....

3   Did it hunt animals?   ....

4   Did the Struthiomimus eat meat?   ....

5   Could it run quickly?   ....

4 Read and complete the chart.

Sauropods were very big dinosaurs. They had four legs, long necks and small heads. They lived on land. They couldn't swim and they couldn't fly. They didn't hunt animals and they didn't eat meat. They ate plants.

Some Pterosaurs were very big and some were small. They lived in the air and they could fly. They had two legs and big wings. They could swim and they hunted fish in the sea. They ate insects, too.

	Where did they live?	Could they swim?	Could they fly?	How many legs did they have?	What did they eat?
Sauropods	on land				
Pterosaurs					

5 Read and write about Theropods.

	Where did they live?	Could they swim?	Could they fly?	How many legs did they have?	What did they eat?
Theropods	on land	No	No	Two big legs, two small legs.	Other dinosaurs, insects and eggs.

Many Theropods were small but some were very big.

They lived ....

....

....

....

(13) They went through the town.

① Look and write the numbers.

1  2   3  4   5   6

☐ train station   ☐ market   ☐ bridge

☐ road   ☐ castle   ☐ hotel

② Choose and write the words from Exercise 1.

1 I bought some strawberries and oranges in the .... market ....

2 Last weekend we stayed in the .... next to the museum.

3 King John lived in this ....

4 This is the .... to London.

5 We couldn't get across the river because there wasn't a ....

6 The .... wasn't very busy because there weren't many trains yesterday.

③ Look and circle.

1  (around)   in   through   4    in   through   across

2  past   through   across   5    around   along   past

3  along   past   around

4 Read and draw the route. Then answer the question.

Claudia and Magnus are here.

After a week, Magnus and Claudia were better. They were ready to leave their hotel. They walked along the road.

It was a hot day. Magnus was thirsty but they walked past the café. They didn't have time to stop for a drink.

They walked around the castle and across the bridge.

They walked quickly through the park.

Then they had to run because they were late. They could see their train. Luckily, they had their tickets because they bought them yesterday.

Where are they going? ....

5 How did the dog get to the farm? Look, choose and write.

forest ~~road~~ house river lake

1 The dog walked across the ....road.......

2 It went ....

3 ....

4 ....

5 ....

6 Choose and write about your journey to school.

along past through across around

1 I .go..............................

2 I ....

3 I ....

14 How much were the tickets?

1 Choose and write.

seat   carriages   ~~luggage~~   searching   look after   money

1 Please can you help me carry my ....luggage........ to the train station?

2 I sit next to my friend Penny at school. Her .... is next to mine.

3 I sometimes .... my little sister in the afternoons.

4 Those children can't find their dog and they're .... for it in the park.

5 I'm going to the bank. I need some ....

6 It's a very long train. It's got ten ....

2 Write questions and answers. M = Mother D = Daughter

shoes ✔ €40
binoculars ✔ €15
torch ✔ €8
sunglasses ✔ €12
guitar ✔ €35
watch ✔ €28

M: How much money did you have?   **D:** I had 150 euros.

M: (1) How much were the shoes?   **D:** They were forty euros.

M: (2) ....   **D:** ....

M: (3) ....   **D:** ....

M: (4) ....   **D:** ....

M: (5) ....   **D:** ....

M: (6) ....   **D:** ....

M: How much money have you got now?   **D:** I've got ....

3 Look, choose and write.

1 There ...are a lot of....... people.

   a ~~are a lot of~~   **b** is a lot of   **c** aren't many

2 There .... empty seats.

   a isn't much   **b** aren't many   **c** are a lot of

3 There .... men.

   a aren't many   **b** is a lot of   **c** are a lot of

4 There .... women.

   a aren't many   **b** isn't many   **c** are a lot of

5 There .... luggage.

   a is a lot of   **b** aren't many   **c** isn't much

6 There .... money.

   a isn't much   **b** aren't many   **c** is a lot of

④ **Look and write True or False.**

1 There are a lot of eggs. ....False........

2 There isn't much spaghetti. ....

3 There aren't many carrots. ....

4 There is a lot of milk. ....

5 There isn't much chicken. ....

6 There isn't much cheese. ....

7 There aren't many biscuits. ....

⑤ **Look at Exercise 4 and write There's a lot of... , There's a little...
or There are a few... .**

1 ......There are a few...... eggs.

2 .... spaghetti.

3 .... carrots.

4 .... milk.

5 .... chicken.

6 .... cheese.

7 .... biscuits.

⑥ **Circle and write much or many.**

There is / are a lot of spaghetti but there aren't / isn't **(1)** .... eggs. There isn't / aren't
(2) .... milk and there isn't / aren't **(3)** .... cheese. There is / are a lot of
chicken. There isn't / aren't **(4)** .... biscuits, but there is / are a lot of carrots.

15 I heard something!

1 **Find, circle and write the six food words.**

e	r	g	e	a	s	f	k	c
u	p	e	a	s	m	w	s	a
l	u	y	i	t	o	f	t	b
n	i	w	t	e	s	e	e	b
p	i	v	e	a	t	y	w	a
s	x	u	h	k	e	w	z	g
c	h	i	p	s	r	i	c	e

1 ...peas...............
2 ....
3 ....
4 ....
5 ....
6 ....

2 **Look and answer the questions.**

1 What's the woman eating?
She's eating pizza and salad.

2 What's the boy eating?
....
....

3 What's the girl eating?
....
....

4 What's the man eating?
....
....

3 **Look at Exercise 2 and circle.**

1 The man isn't drinking anybody / anything.

2 The girl isn't talking to anybody / anything.

3 There's something / nothing on top of the luggage.

4 There's something / nothing on the seat next to the woman.

5 Nobody / Somebody is looking out of the window.

6 Nobody / Somebody is reading the newspaper.

4 Read and match.

1 They said   nobody saw them.

2 They asked   anything to do.

3 They didn't see   nothing about the toucan.

4 They hid and   somebody for help.

5 They didn't have   something to eat.

6 They bought   anybody outside the door.

5 Choose and write.

1 Can you see ...anybody... in the carriage?
   a nothing   **b** nobody   **c** (anybody)

2 I can see Dr Wild with the luggage.
   There's .... with her.
   a nobody   **b** anything   **c** anybody

3 Jack is talking to .... on his mobile.
   a somebody   **b** anything   **c** anybody

4 He says he didn't eat .... for breakfast.
   a somebody   **b** nobody   **c** anything

5 He's hungry. He wants .... to eat.
   a anything   **b** something   **c** nothing

6 He looked for some food in his bag but there's
   .... in it.
   a somebody   **b** nothing   **c** anything

6 Write sentences.

1 not sit next to/anybody   He _isn't sitting next to anybody._ .

2 play with/something   She ....

3 phone/somebody   She ....

4 not eat/anything   He ....

5 not read/anything   She ....

6 not listen to/anybody   He ....

I'd like chips.

16 SKILLS

Writing Class: *first, then, afterwards, finally*

① **Choose, write and match.**

Afterwards   First   Finally   ~~Last week~~   Then

1 ....Last week.......... our class went to   lunch in a café.
2 .... we walked around the   to the shop.
3 .... we ate   the Great Park.
4 .... we visited   castle.
5 .... we went   Windsor.

② **Look and correct the sentences.**

1 Last month we went to London.   Last month, we went to York. ....
2 First we went to the museum and   ....
   looked at the cars.
3 Then we had lunch in a café.   ....
4 Afterwards we visited the library.   ....
5 Finally we walked along the river.   ....

③ **Write a report about a school trip.**

Write about:

• when and where you went.

• four things you did in the order you did them.

• a place you visited, the food you ate, two things you did.

Our school trip to ....

First ....

Then ....

Afterwards ....

Finally ....

④ Choose and complete the table.

cake   milk   chicken   peaches   carrots   ice cream   water   steak   potatoes   orange juice
peas   ~~stew~~   cherries   apples   chocolate

Meat	Vegetables	Drinks	Fruit	Sweet
stew				

⑤ Read and circle.

What would you like?

    I'd like stew, cabbage and rice, please.

And to drink?

    I'll have orange juice, please.

Would you like anything else?

    Yes, I'd like chocolate cake, please.
Thank you.

⑥ Read and write the questions.

1 What would you like?

I'd like chicken and salad, please.

2 ....

I'll have milk, please.

3 ....

Yes, I'd like strawberries, please.

FlyHigh File: London bus tour

1 Choose and write.

double-decker bus   Big Wheel   art gallery   hill   theatre   ~~tower~~   cathedral

1 This isn't a house but it is very tall.   tower

2 Singers and dancers sometimes work here.   ....

3 You can see lots of paintings here.   ....

4 People often go here on Sundays.   ....

5 It's fun to go on this.
   You sit in a seat and go very high!   ....

6 This is a big bus with stairs and lots of seats.   ....

7 It's hard to walk up here but it's fun to run down. ....

2 Read, choose and write. Then number the photos in order.

cathedral   theatre   River   ~~double-decker bus~~   art gallery

a

The Tate Modern
is an art gallery.

b PALLADIUM

The Sound of MUSIC

The Palladium
is a theatre.

c

This is the
River Thames.

d

St Paul's is a
cathedral.

1

e

The Tower of
London is very old.

Hello, I'm Eve. I went to London last month with my school. London is the capital of England. It's a beautiful city with lots of things to see and do. We went on a tour of the city on a **(1)** double-decker bus.
First we went to St Paul's. That's a beautiful **(2)** .... Then we saw the Tower of London.
There were lots of big black birds in the gardens. We also saw the Palladium. That's a famous
(3) .... Then we walked around the Tate Modern. That's an **(4)** ....
Finally we went on a boat along the **(5)** .... Thames. We had a great time!

③ Read Exercise 2 again and correct the sentences.

1 London is the capital of Italy.   London is the capital of England.

2 They went on a tour in a car.   ....

3 They saw some black cats
   at the Tower of London.   ....

4 They fell in the River Thames.   ....

④ Read and label the map.

Blackhorse Road   Sunny Bridge   Bushy Park   Whitewater River   Toy Museum
~~Green Street~~   castle   art gallery

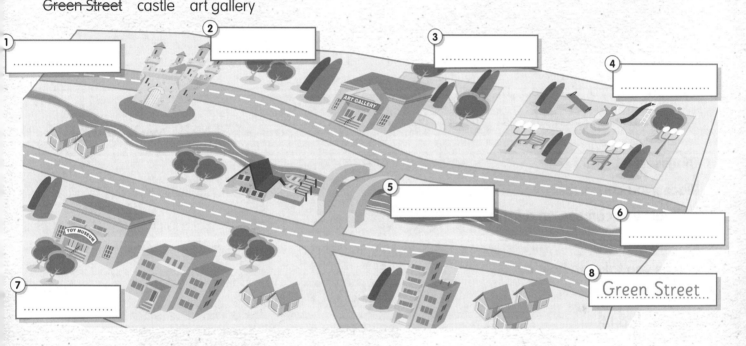

Last weekend my friend and I walked around our town. First we went to the Toy Museum in Green Street. That was great. We saw lots of old dolls and cars there.

Then we went across Sunny Bridge to Blackhorse Road and went to the castle there. The castle has a very high tower.

Then we went to Bushy Park. There's an art gallery there with lots of nice paintings.

Finally we got on a boat and went along Whitewater River.

⑤ What about you? Complete the chart.

What about your town? Are there any interesting places to visit? Where are they?

Name of place	Name of street

The FlyHigh Review

① Circle and write. Then add your own words.

```
t  e  h  m  o  n  e  y  n  c  s
r  a  o  g  b  s  x  l  s  o  c
i  r  r  d  u  c  k  f  t  l  a
c  a  s  t  l  e  j  z  e  d  r
e  c  e  r  l  u  g  g  a  g  e
o  h  m  u  s  e  u  m  k  m  d
n  e  r  v  o  u  s  j  o  w  l
```

Your words

1 Illnesses   earache ....

2 Places you can visit   ....

3 Animals you can see on a farm   ....

4 Food   ....

5 Things you take on holiday   ....

6 Birds   ....

7 How you can feel   ....

② Circle five differences and write.   ~~stew~~   potatoes   cabbage   water   peas

Before

After

1   There was a lot of stew.   There isn't much stew now.

2   ....

3   ....

4   ....

5   ....

③ Look and correct the sentences.

1 There was something in front of the hotel. _There wasn't anything in front of the hotel._

2 There were a lot of cars on the road. ....

3 There was a bridge past the river. ....

4 Somebody was on the bridge. ....

5 The road went through the hotel. ....

6 There weren't many people in the market. ....

④ Write about you. Use could or couldn't.

1 (talk) When I was one, _I couldn't talk._   **4** (swim) When I was four, ...

2 (sing) When I was two, ...   **5** (dance) When I was five, ...

3 (run) When I was three, ...   **6** (climb) When I was six, ...

My English

How did I do? Write OK / Well / Very well.

1 Learn with Oscar He drove/it couldn't sleep/It's past the shop/Nobody's got much rice ....

2 New words cow/confused/headache/dinosaur/castle/luggage/steak/theatre ....

3 Writing Letter .... Report ....

4 Conversations Apologising .... Ordering food ....

5 Projects Making a dinosaur chart .... Making a town chart ....

Alice in Wonderland

① Choose and write.

hare ~~place~~ polite tea wide angrily wine

1 Where shall I sit? There isn't a ...._place_........ for me.

2 Sometimes my parents have a glass of red .... with their dinner.

3 That's a very big rabbit. I think it's a ....

4 You must speak nicely to your teachers and be ....

5 I like milk and sugar in my cup of ....

6 When you are very surprised, you open your eyes ....

7 'No! You mustn't do that. You are a bad child!' the old woman said ....

② Read The Mad Hatter's Tea Party on pages 52–53 of your Pupil's Book. Tick the correct picture.

1 (a)   (b) ✔

2 (a)   (b)

3 (a)   (b)

4 (a)   (b)

3 Circle the correct sentence.

1 **a** The Mad Hatter, the March Hare and the mouse want Alice to sit at the table.

  (b) The Mad Hatter, the March Hare and the mouse don't want Alice to sit at the table.

2 **a** The mouse doesn't say anything.

  b The mouse talks a lot.

3 **a** Alice doesn't think the Mad Hatter and the March Hare are very polite.

  b Alice thinks the Mad Hatter and the March Hare are very polite.

4 **a** Alice cuts her hair.

  b Alice doesn't cut her hair.

5 **a** The Mad Hatter's watch has numbers.

  b The Mad Hatter's watch has the days of the week.

6 **a** The March Hare puts the watch in his tea.

  b The March Hare puts the watch in his cake.

4 Write True or False.

1 There was a small table under the tree. ....False.......

2 The Mad Hatter invited Alice to tea. ....

3 They drink wine. ....

4 The March Hare put butter on the Mad Hatter's watch. ....

5 The Mad Hatter thinks his watch is strange. ....

6 Alice thinks the watch is strange. ....

5 Match the sentences with the same meaning.

1 There aren't any places.

2 We didn't invite you to tea.

3 That wasn't very polite of you.

4 The Mad Hatter opened his eyes very wide.

a You didn't speak nicely.

b He was very surprised.

c We didn't ask you to come.

d There isn't anywhere to sit.

17 Is it yours?

① Read and colour.

The girl's got orange gloves.
She's got a green scarf.
She's got pink trainers.

The boy's got a brown belt.
He's got a green jacket.
He's got a red tie.

② Look at Exercise 1 again. Write his or hers.

1 The gloves are ....hers............ .

2 The tie is ....

3 The jacket is ....

4 The trainers are ....

5 The belt is ....

6 The scarf is ....

③ Look at Exercise 1. Circle and answer.

1 Whose binoculars is it / (are they)? ....They're his............

2 Whose hat is it / are they? ....

3 Whose torch is it / are they? ....

4 Whose sweater is it / are they? ....

5 Whose glasses is it / are they? ....

6 Whose boots is it / are they? ....

(4) Rewrite the sentences. Use mine, yours, his, hers, ours, theirs.

1 Is this your bag? ......Is this yours?......

2 No, but that's my camera. ....

3 They're our shoes. ....

4 That's her mobile. ....

5 We can't find his ticket. ....

6 Have you got their laptop? ....

(5) Choose and write.

mine   glasses   are   his   ~~is~~   hers   Whose   yours

Mum: Look at this mess. Whose belt
(1) ..is.............. this? Is it
(2) ...., Danny?

Danny: No, it isn't **(3)** .... It's Elaine's.

Mum: What about these **(4)** ....?

Danny: They're **(5)** ...., too.

Mum: These trainers look like Ivan's.

Danny: Yes, I think they're **(6)** ....

Mum: **(7)** .... gloves are these?

Danny: They **(8)** .... yours, Mum!

(6) Look, write and match.

ⓐ ⓑ ⓒ ⓓ ⓔ

1 ....Whose dog is it?............   a   ....

2 ....   b   ....

3   c   ....

4 ....   d   It's ours. ....

5 ....   e   ....

18 You don't have to shout!

1 Match the opposites. Then choose and write.

1 The children ...leave........... home at five past eight and
..................................at school at quarter to nine.

2 The lessons .... at nine o'clock and ....
at three.

3 The children .... their bags to school every morning
and .... them home at the end of the day.

4 In class, they sometimes ....their pencil and have to
.... another one.

leave — find
start ⟍ arrive
lose — bring
take — finish

2 Read and circle.

Yesterday I **(1)** (went)/ looked to London with my family. The trip **(2)** landed / started well.
We **(3)** left / needed home early and **(4)** arrived / asked there about ten o'clock.
We **(5)** helped / visited the Tower of London. Then we **(6)** stopped / had a picnic lunch in
a nice park.

After lunch there was a disaster! My mum **(7)** lost / came her bag with her money and
mobile phone. We went to the police station and **(8)** met / dropped a man at the front
door. He **(9)** had / made my mum's bag! He said he **(10)** found / wanted it under a seat
in the park! My mum was very happy. She **(11)** stayed / took us to a café and we had a
wonderful dinner before we came home. The day **(12)** brought / finished happily.

3 Choose and write. Use have to or has to.

feed the cat   go shopping   water the plants   tidy her room   ~~wash the dishes~~   make my bed

1  We ..have to wash the dishes...

4 My mum and dad ....

2  My friend ....

5 I ....

3 My brother ....

6 They ....

(4) **Choose and write. Use have to or has to.**

run   pack   ~~learn~~   buy   walk   throw   listen   invite

1 We want to speak English well.

.....You have to learn..... the new words.

.... to your teacher.

2 He wants to play basketball.

.... fast.

.... the ball well.

3 She wants to have a picnic.

.... some friends.

.... some food.

4 They want to stay with their grandma.

.... their bags.

.... to their grandma's house.

(5) **Look and write the questions. Then answer.**

1 be on a lead   Does it have to be on a lead?   No, it doesn't.

2 walk with their bikes   Do they ....   No, ...

3 put the litter in the bin ....

4 stay off the grass   ....

5 wear a uniform   ....

6 water the plants   ....

(6) **What about you? Complete using have to / don't have to.**

1 ....I have to.... do my homework.

2 .... learn Maths.

3 .... wear black shoes at school.

4 .... arrive at school on time.

5 .... learn a musical instrument.

6 .... go to school on Saturday.

19 Dr Wild went to the bank to get some money.

① Complete and find the hidden word. Then answer the question below.

1 You can watch a film here.
2 You can read books here.
3 You can hire a car here.
4 You can get money here.
5 You can have lunch here.
6 You can send a parcel here.

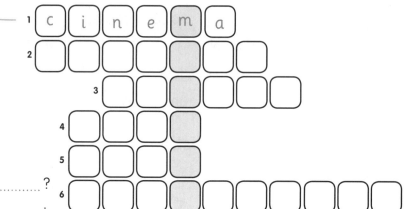

| 1 | c | i | n | e | m | a |

What can you do at the .... ?
You can ....

② Look, write and tick.

garage   café   ~~supermarket~~   post office   pet shop   library

1 He went to the _supermarket_

to buy some apples. ....
to get some money. ....

2 He went to the ....

to hire a car. ....
to get some water. ....

3 He went to the ....

to get a parcel. ....
to send a letter. ....

4 He went to the ....

to read a newspaper. ....
to find a book. ....

5 He went to the ....

to have a drink. ....
to eat a sandwich. ....

6 He went to the ....

to look at the snakes. ....
to buy a rabbit. ....

③ Read and match.

1 They stopped the car
2 I turned on the radio
3 He emailed his teacher
4 You went to the playground
5 We bought some bread
6 She made a birthday card

a to make sandwiches.
b to play on the swings.
c to look at the map.
d to ask about the homework.
e to send to her aunt.
f to listen to some music.

(4) **Look, match and write.**

tidy my clothes   have a shower   ~~cut the grass~~   cook the dinner   watch TV

(a)   (b)   (c)   (d)   (e)

1 [c] I'm going to the garden _to cut the grass_ .

2 [ ] I'm going to the bedroom ....

3 [ ] I'm going to the bathroom ....

4 [ ] I'm going to the kitchen ....

5 [ ] I'm going to the living room ....

(5) **Look and write.**

Shopping list

1 bank — get some money

2 post office — send a parcel

3 toy shop — buy a present

4 supermarket — buy some milk

5 library — hire a DVD

1 she/go/bank/money

First _she went to the bank to get some money_ .

2 she/go/post office/parcel

Then _she_ ....

3 she/go/toy shop/present

Afterwards ....

4 she/go/supermarket/milk

Next ....

5 she/go/library/DVD

Finally ....

(6) **Complete with your own ideas.**

1 I went upstairs to ....

2 I phoned my friend to ....

3 We went to the park to ....

4 I asked for some money to ....

5 We needed the binoculars to ....

20 I arrive at twenty to nine.

SKILLS

Writing Class: writing the time

① **Look and match.**

a
b
c
d

1 It's five past six. | c |
2 It's quarter past twelve. | |
3 It's ten to four. | |
4 It's twenty-five to three. | |

② **Look, circle and write.**

1 We have an English lesson at   quarter / ~~twenty~~ to .... *eleven* ....

2 We go to the playground at   five / ten past ....

3 I arrive home at   twenty / twenty-five past ....

4 I do my homework at   quarter / ten to ....

③ **Number the sentences in order.**

	School finishes at twenty past three.
	We have lunch at ten past twelve.
1	Every day I leave home at half past eight.
	The afternoon lessons start at one o'clock.

	The first lesson starts at five past nine.
	After school I go to the swimming pool for my swimming lesson.
	I arrive at school at quarter to nine.

④ **Write a composition about your school day.**

Write what time:

• you leave home and arrive at school.

• you have lunch and what you eat.

• you finish school and what you do after school.

My school day

Every day I ....

....

....

....

....

5 Read and number the pictures.

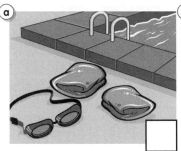 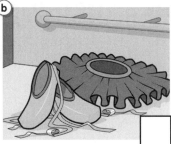  

a [ ] b [ ] c [1] d [ ]

1
I have to go to the music room now.
I've got a keyboard lesson.
It starts at twenty-five to three.

3
I have to go to the swimming pool now.
I've got a swimming lesson.
It starts at quarter to six.

2
I have to go to the playing field now.
I've got a football match.
It starts at half past five.

4
I have to go to the school hall now.
I've got a dance lesson.
It starts at five past twelve.

6 Match and number in order. Then write.

[ ] I've got a   **a** for?   **1** I have to go to the swimming pool now.

[ ] At quarter   **b** it start?   **2** ....

[ ] What   **c** swimming lesson.   **3** ....

[1] I have to go to the ⌐ **d** later.   **4** ....

[ ] See you   └ **e** swimming pool now.   **5** ....

[ ] What time does   **f** to six.   **6** ....

7 Choose and write.

ten past four   ~~music room~~   trumpet lesson

1 I have to go to the music room now.   What for?

2 I've got a ....   What time does it start?

3 ....   OK. See you later.

FlyHigh File: Clothes through the ages

1 Look and label.

apron   dress   ~~cap~~   tunic   trainers

a   cap

b

c

d

21st century   18th century   14th century   12th century

2 Look at Exercise 1 and write.

1 21st century The cap is from the twenty-first century.
2 14th century ....
3 18th century ....
4 12th century ....
5 21st century ....

3 Look at Exercise 1 again and write.

1 The boy lived in the _twelfth_ century. He wore _a tunic, a belt, trousers and shoes_.
2 The man lived in the .... century. He wore ....
3 The woman lived in the .... century. She wore ....
4 The girl is living in the .... century. She's wearing ....

4 Read, choose and write.

nurses ~~year~~ name shoes work uniform

Today the fashions change every **(1)** .....year..... and people wear many different styles of clothes. You can choose the clothes you wear. However, some people have to wear special clothes when they go to **(2)** .... They have to wear a **(3)** .... Firefighters, police officers and **(4)** .... all wear uniforms at work. In Britain, many children also have to wear uniforms when they go to school. At most primary schools the children wear a special sweater with the school **(5)** .... and logo on it, with a dark skirt or trousers. At secondary school the children have to wear a school tie and a jacket called a blazer with a skirt or trousers and brown or black **(6)** .... They also have a special PE kit for games with a shirt, shorts and socks in the school colours.

5 Read Exercise 4 again and answer the questions.

1 Who wears uniforms? ....

2 Do all children in Britain wear school uniforms? ....

3 What does a primary school child's sweater have on it? ....

4 Who wears a school tie? ....

5 What's a blazer? ....

6 What's special about the PE kit? ....

6 Read and tick Jason's favourite clothes.

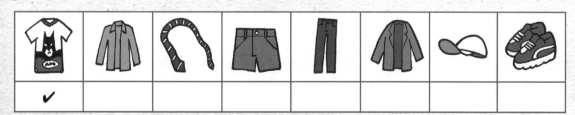

I'm Jason and I've got some great clothes. My favourite clothes are my brown T-shirt and my green shorts. There's a picture of Batman on my T-shirt. I also like my grey jacket. I've got a really cool cap, which I wear in the summer, and I've got cool trainers too.

21 The red van is faster!

1 Choose and write.

~~motorbike~~   van   fire engine   scooter   airport   helicopter

1 It has two wheels and can go very fast.   ......motorbike......
2 Lots of people visit this place to go on holiday.   ....
3 Firefighters drive it.   ....
4 It flies in the air.   ....
5 It has two wheels and doesn't go very fast.   ....
6 It's bigger than a car and has four wheels.   ....

2 Look and write. Use words from Exercise 2.

1 dirty/clean

The van is dirtier than the car.

The car is

2 big/small

....

....

3 fast/slow

....

....

4 old/new

....

....

3 Write True or False.

1 Helicopters are bigger than cars.

....True....

2 Cars are slower than bikes.

....

3 Motorbikes are faster than bikes.

....

4 Ambulances are smaller than scooters.

....

5 Scooters are smaller than vans.

....

6 Fire engines are bigger than motorbikes.

....

62

④ **Look, read and write.**

Bella Dad Mum Simon

This is my family. Mum is much **(1)** ___shorter___ (short) than Dad. My brother Simon is thirteen but he's **(2)** .... (tall) than my Mum. Simon is **(3)** .... (old) than my sister Bella. She's five and she's **(4)** .... (young) than me. Bella is **(5)** .... (happy) than Simon because she's got a **(6)** .... (big) ball! Simon and Dad love playing football but Simon's clothes are always **(7)** .... (dirty) than Dad's.

⑤ **Read Exercise 4 again. Correct the sentences.**

1 My dad is older of me.   ...My dad is older than me....................
2 My sister is young than me.   ....
3 My mum shorter than my dad.   ....
4 I'm tall than my sister.   ....
5 My bedroom is biger than my sister's. ....
6 I'm happyer today than I was yesterday. ....

⑥ **What about you? Write full answers.**

1 Are you older than your teacher?   ...No, I'm younger than my teacher........
2 Are you taller than your dad?   ....
3 Is your school smaller than your house? ....
4 Is your nose bigger than an elephant's? ....
5 Are your feet smaller than a cat's feet? ....
6 Is a giraffe shorter than you?   ....

22 They are the silliest people in the world!

① Choose and write.

catch   runner   silly   ~~noisy~~   light

1 'Be quiet!' said the teacher. 'Don't be ..... noisy ....'
2 Feathers aren't heavy. They're ....
3 My little sister is only one and she can't .... a ball.
4 I like the clowns at the circus. They're funny and .... too.
5 My friend is good at sport. He's a very fast ....

② Write the sentences in the correct order.

1 boy / He's / class / cleverest / the / my / in
   ..... He's the cleverest boy in my class. ....
2 in / brother / is / person / the / My / noisiest / family / our
   ....
3 are / in / the / the / world / heaviest / Whales / animals
   ....
4 Europe / The / longest / in / Volga / is / the / river
   ....
5 My / has / in / friend / hair / got / the / school / longest / the
   ....
6 fastest / in / the / runner / I'm / class / my
   ....

③ Look and answer.

1 Is David the shortest? ..Yes, he is. ....
2 Is Carol the tallest? ....
3 Is Carol slower than Matt? ....

4 Is David the fastest runner? ....
5 Has Carol got the longest hair? ....
6 Has Matt got the shortest hair? ....

4 Correct one word.

1 He's got the ~~biggiest~~ hat. ....biggest.........

2 My dad is heaviest than my mum. ....

3 They're the sillest people in the world. ....

4 The clown was the funiest person in the show.

....

5 My brother is noisiest than me. ....

5 Read and write.

Mountains in Europe

The Elbrus is 5,642 metres high.

Mont Blanc is 4,807 metres high.

The Dom is 4,545 metres high.

1 ....The Dom........... is a high mountain.

2 .... is higher than The Dom.

3 .... is the highest mountain.

4 Mont Blanc is higher than ....

5 The Elbrus ....

6 Look and write sentences.

| Ben | Betsy | Tony | Katya | Ron | Poppy |

1 strong Ron is the strongest child in the class.

2 silly ....

3 short ....

4 tall ....

5 long/hair ....

6 short/hair ....

7 Write about your friends in your class.

1 tall/girl The tallest girl is ....

2 short/girl ....

3 tall/boy ....

4 short/boy ....

5 fast/runner ....

6 funny/child ....

7 strong/child ....

23 Oscar has got the most comfortable bed!

① Circle the correct word.

1 The seats on the bus were small. They weren't very **comfortable** / exciting.
2 My bed's comfortable. It's very dangerous / soft.
3 It's modern / dangerous to swim in the sea when it's stormy.
4 It's fun to go tobogganing / exciting in the snow.
5 I saw my favourite singer in town last night! It was so soft / exciting!
6 My grandfather doesn't wear modern / dangerous clothes. He likes old clothes.
7 I would like a new phone with a camera but they're very soft / expensive.

② Complete the chart.

expensive	more expensive	the most expensive
	cheaper	
dangerous		
		the most beautiful
	more interesting	
exciting		
	more boring	
		the funniest
comfortable		
	softer	
modern		

③ Look and write. Then answer.

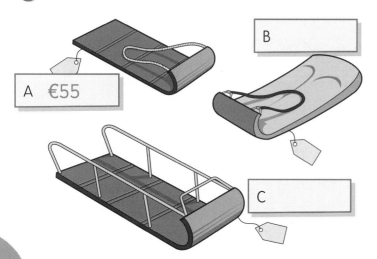

A €55
B
C

Toboggan A is fifty-five euros.
Toboggan B is eighty-nine euros.
Toboggan C is one hundred and fifty euros.

1 Which toboggan is the cheapest? ....A....
2 Which one is the most expensive? ....
3 Is toboggan B more expensive than A?
....
4 Is toboggan C cheaper than B?
....

④ Look and write.

	Is it comfortable?
Bed A	✔
Bed B	✔ ✔
Bed C	✔ ✔ ✔

comfortable

1 Bed A is a .... comfortable .... bed .

2 Bed B is more .... than bed A .

3 Bed C is the .... bed .

	Is it interesting?
Book A	✔
Book B	✔ ✔
Book C	✔ ✔ ✔

interesting

1 Book A ....

2 Book B ....

3 Book C ....

	Is it modern?
Living room A	✔
Living room B	✔ ✔
Living room C	✔ ✔ ✔

modern

1 Living room A ....

2 Living room B ....

3 Living room C ....

⑤ Complete the sentences about Hotel Posh.
Then write about Hotel Trendy using the opposite adjectives.

Hotel Posh

1 Hotel Posh is ...older... (old) than Hotel Trendy.

2 It's .... (big) than Hotel Trendy.

3 It's .... (noisy) than Hotel Trendy.

5 It's .... (expensive) hotel in town.

6 It's .... (bad) hotel in town.

Hotel Trendy

1 Hotel Trendy is more modern than Hotel Posh.

2 It's ....

3 It's ....

5 It's ....

6 It's ....

⑥ Answer the questions.

What do you think is the most ...

1 dangerous animal? ..I think the most dangerous animal is..............................

2 exciting sport? ....

3 interesting lesson? ....

4 expensive thing in your school? ....

Which bike do you like best?

Writing Class: adjective order

(1) Choose and write.

~~grey~~ ~~amazing~~ ~~long~~ purple expensive orange small beautiful white great
short interesting dangerous big tall black high yellow

Opinion	Size	Colour
amazing	long	grey

(2) Choose words from Exercise 1. Write them in the correct order.

1 He's got ....an amazing.. , ... , ... car.

2 I saw .... , ... , ... bird yesterday.

3 It's .... , ... , ... bike.

(3) Write an advertisement.

- Choose a name.
- Write about your opinion, the size and the colour.
- Compare it to the other bikes in the shop. Is it the biggest, the fastest or the cheapest bike?

The .... is a fantastic bike!
It's ....
....
....
....

4 **Look and tick.**

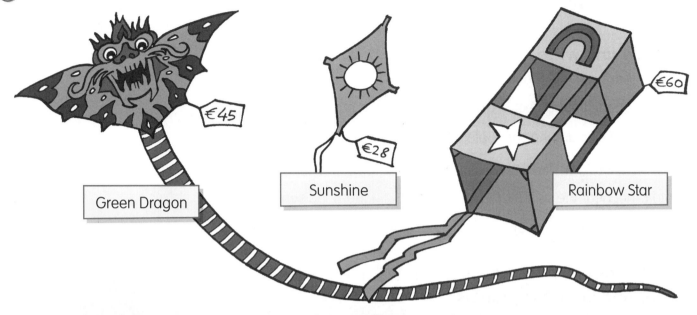

Green Dragon €45

Sunshine €28

Rainbow Star €60

	Green Dragon	Sunshine	Rainbow Star
the most expensive			✔
the cheapest			
the biggest			
the smallest			
the longest tail			
the shortest tail			
the strongest			

5 **Choose, write and answer.**

has   exciting   best   ~~most~~

1 Which kite is the ___most___ expensive? ....

2 Which one .... got the longest tail? ....

3 Which kite do you think is the most .... ? ....

4 Which one do you like .... ? ....

6 **Choose your favourite kite and write.**

I like the .... kite best.

It's the .... , the .... and ....

FlyHigh File: Planets

1) Choose and write.

stars   furthest   rock   ~~gas~~   rings   ice

1 Some planets are made of ___gas___ but earth is made of _____ .

2 There are circles around some planets. The circles are called _____ .

3 When water is very cold it's _____ .

4 Pluto is not near the sun. It's the _____ from the sun.

5 At night you can see lots of _____ in the sky.

2) Put the letters in the correct order and label the planets.

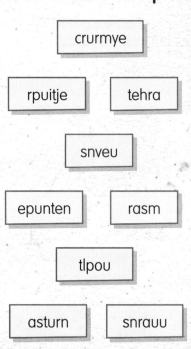

crurmye

rpuitje   tehra

snveu

epunten   rasm

tlpou

asturn   snrauu

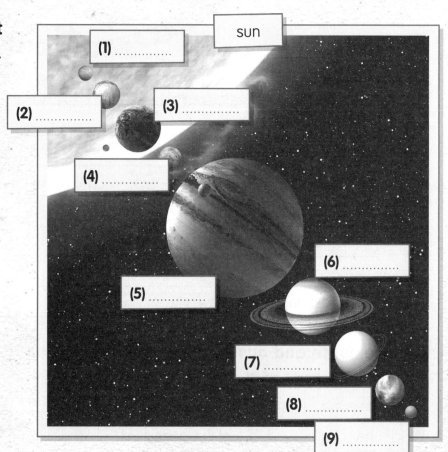

sun

(1) _____

(2) _____

(3) _____

(4) _____

(5) _____

(6) _____

(7) _____

(8) _____

(9) _____

3) Complete the sentences.

1 hot   Venus   _is the hottest planet_ .

2 big   Jupiter _____ .

3 cold   Pluto _____ .

4 near   Mercury _____ to the sun.

5 far   Pluto _____ from the sun.

6 small   Pluto _____ .

④ Read and answer the questions.

The moon is not a planet. It goes around our planet earth. It's made of rock. There are seas on the moon but there isn't any water in the seas.

There isn't any weather on the moon. It isn't windy there and it never snows or rains. The moon is smaller than earth. Sometimes it looks big, sometimes it looks small. When it's big and round, it's called a full moon. When it's very small, it's called a new moon.

The first men on the moon were Neil Armstrong and Edwin Aldrin. They landed on the moon on July 20th 1969 and they walked around for two hours.

1 What's the moon made of? .....It's made of rock......

2 Can you swim in the seas on the moon? ....

3 Does it rain on the moon? ....

4 Which moon looks bigger, a full moon or a new moon? ....

5 When did Neil Armstrong and Edwin Aldrin land on the moon? ....

⑤ Look and write.

	Mercury	Mars	Saturn	Uranus
Made of	rock	rock	gas	gas
Temperature	hot	cold	very cold	very cold
Other information	It looks like the moon.	It's red.	It's got rings of ice.	It's got five big moons.

1 ....Uranus.... has got five big .... It's made of gas and it's ....

2 .... is a red planet. It's .... and it's made of rock.

3 .... looks like the moon. It is .... and it's made of ....

4 .... is .... and it's made of .... It's got rings of ....

① **Complete and find the hidden word. Then complete the sentence below.**

1 Something you wear on your head.
2 Something you wear around your neck to keep you warm.
3 You wear this like a coat.
4 Something you can wear only with a shirt.
5 You wear this when you cook.
6 Something you wear to hold your trousers up.
7 Girls wear this.
8 You wear these on your hands

You wear these on your ....

¹ h a t
²
³ t
⁴
⁵ p
⁶
⁷ s
⁸

② **Match and write questions and answers.**

① ② ③ ④

a b c d

1 ....Whose ambulance is it?.................... | b | ....It's theirs.............

2 .... | | ....

3 .... | | ....

4 .... | | ....

3 Read and write.

| Pluto -230°C | Uranus -200°C | Bike 500€ | Scooter 5,000€ |

| Neptune -210°C | Motorbike 20,000€ |

Uranus is a **cold** planet.

1 Neptune is ...colder than... Uranus.

2 Pluto is .... planet.

The bike is **expensive**.

3 The scooter is .... bike.

4 The motorbike is ....

4 Write sentences about a camping trip.

1 arrive early/put up the tents ......The family arrived early to put up the tents.

2 look for some wood/make a fire. The children ....

3 need some fish/cook for dinner. They ....

4 bring a guitar/sing songs in the evening. They ....

5 take binoculars/watch the birds. They ....

5 Write questions about your English lessons. Then answer.

~~learn~~ play work paint listen to your teacher games ~~new words~~ pictures hard

1 Do you have to learn new words?   Yes, we do.

2

3

4

5

My English

How did I do? Write OK/Well/Very well.

1 **Learn with Oscar** It's mine/we have to leave now to catch the train/
It's the most comfortable bed ....

2 **New words** scarf/arrive/bank/apron/van/noisy/expensive/planet ....

3 **Writing** Composition ....   Advertisement ....

4 **Conversations** Explaining arrangements ....   Comparing and contrasting ....

5 **Projects** Writing about your favourite clothes ....   Describing the planets ....

The Prince and the Pauper

① Put the letters in the correct order and write.

1 The king and queen live in a ...palace... (lpacea).
2 She opened the .... (tega) and walked into the garden.
3 The .... (doleris) wore a red jacket and black trousers and he carried a gun.
4 A .... (garbeg) asked me for some money this morning.
5 The rich man had a big house. A lot of .... (venstars) worked there for him.
6 The .... (pepura) had no money and his clothes were old and dirty.

② Read The Prince and the Pauper on pages 76–77 of your Pupil's Book. Number the pictures in the correct order.

3 Look at Exercise 2, choose and write.

a ~~Tom was a pauper. He went to the palace every day.~~

b The Prince and Tom changed clothes.

c A servant brought lots of good food for Tom to eat.

d Tom saw Prince Edward in the palace. A soldier hit him!

e The Prince had an idea. He wanted to be a pauper and play with other boys.

f The Prince was angry with the soldier. He invited Tom into the palace.

g The Prince ran out of the palace. Tom didn't know what to do.

h The Prince and Tom talked. The Prince liked Tom's stories.

Picture One: Tom was a pauper. He went to the palace every day.

Picture Two: ....

Picture Three: ....

Picture Four: ....

Picture Five: ....

Picture Six: ....

Picture Seven: ....

Picture Eight: ....

4 Write True or False.

1 Tom's home was the palace.   False

2 Tom's family was rich.   ....

3 Tom sometimes asked other people for money.   ....

4 Prince Edward kicked Tom.   ....

5 The Prince had lots of friends.   ....

6 The Prince wanted to be a poor boy for a day. ....

5 Choose and write.

poor   day   ~~lived~~   sisters   servants   room   food   rich   palace   boys

Tom **(1)** lived with his **(2)** ...., his parents and his grandmother in one
(3) .... They were very **(4)** .... and they were always hungry.
Prince Edward lived in a **(5)** .... with his father, the King and lots of
(6) .... They were very **(7)** .... and they always had lots of
(8) .... Tom had friends and he played with them. The Prince didn't have
any friends. There weren't any other **(9)** .... in the palace. The Prince wanted
to live like Tom for a **(10)** ....

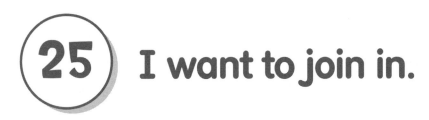

25 I want to join in.

① Choose and write.

costumes   alien   ~~spy~~   superhero   fancy dress   pop star

1 He's wearing a raincoat and a false beard and moustache. Do you think he's a ....spy........ ?

2 I'm reading a book about an .... He comes from the planet Jupiter.

3 We're in the school play. Our mum has to make our ....

4 I like Batman. Who's your favourite .... ?

5 She has singing lessons. She wants to be a ....

6 I'm going to a .... party tonight.

② Look and match.

a He wants to be a photographer.

b I want to be a postman.

c She wants to be a police officer.

d They want to be pop stars.

e We want to be nurses.

76

③ Choose and write.

ride   fly   chase   ~~go~~   play   make

1 ___He wants to go___ on the swing. **4** _____ a sandcastle.

2 _____ her bike. **5** _____ tennis.

3 _____ a kite. **6** _____ the cat.

④ Look and write.

1 play ___He wants to play basketball.___   **4** climb _____

2 go ___They don't___ .   **5** carry _____

3 make _____

⑤ What about you? Answer the questions.

1 What do you want to do after school today? _____

2 What do you want to eat for dinner? _____

3 What do you want to do next weekend? _____

4 Where do you want to go next holiday? _____

26 He likes tobogganing!

1 Find and circle six activities.

1 evening   5 rock climbing   9 surfing

2 (cycling)   6 skateboarding   10 lightning

3 fishing   7 morning   11 wing

4 swing   8 climbing frame   12 ice skating

2 Look and write the words in Exercise 1.

1 _skateboarding_   2 ....   3 ....

4 ....   5 ....   6 ....

3 Look and write using be happy when.

1 My _mum's happy when she's reading_   4 My grandma ....

2 My dad ....   5 The bird ....

3 My brother and sister ....   6 I ....

....

4 Look and write.

1 like ....He doesn't like running.............

2 good at ....She's good at jumping.............

3 like ....

4 good at ....

5 good at ....

6 like ....

7 like ....

8 good at ....

5 Correct the sentences.

1 I happy when I'm cycling. ......I'm happy when I'm cycling..........

2 I'm good at skateboard. ....

3 He's happy when he fishing. ....

4 She don't like rock climbing. ....

5 They're good in ice skating. ....

6 Do you like play volleyball? ....

6 What about you? Complete with your own ideas.

1 I like (+ *something you do with your friends*) ....

2 I'm good at (+ *something you do in the playground*) ....

3 I don't like (+ *something you do every day*) ....

4 I'm not good at (+ *a sport*) ....

5 I feel happy when I'm (+ *something you do at home*) ....

27 What shall we do?

1 **Circle the odd one out.**

1 alien	pop star	~~rescuing~~	superhero
2 borrow	sun	star	moon
3 tie	belt	scarf	escaping
4 niece	hold	nephew	uncle
5 silly	using	funny	noisy
6 behind	along	reaching	across

2 **Write suggestions using the circled words in Exercise 1. Then number the pictures.**

1 What about/the cat? _What about rescuing the cat?_

2 Shall we/a torch? ....

3 What about/through that gate? ....

4 Shall I/the boat for you? ....

5 What about/a spade? ....

6 What about/the bridge before we stop for lunch? ....

3 **Write the words in the correct order.**

> We're lost!

1 to / ask / we / us? / Shall / somebody / help _Shall we ask somebody to help us?_

2 compass? / What / using / about / the ....

3 the / looking / about / map? / at / What ....

4 Shall / now? / go / we / home ....

(4) **Write Shall we or What about and match.**

1 ..... What about ..... going to the toy shop? a OK. I've got my bike.
2 .... take a picnic? b I don't want to. I haven't got any money.
3 .... go cycling? c No, thanks. I don't want to get wet.
4 .... making a fruit cake? d OK. You start counting and we'll hide.
5 .... having a water pistol fight? e OK. We need to buy some flour.
6 .... play Hide and Seek? f Good idea. I'll make some sandwiches.

(5) **Read, match and write.**

1
watching a different film
~~come back tomorrow~~

a
Oh no! It's raining.

Shall we .... ?

What about .... ?

2
jump across
finding a bridge

b
Oh no! We're late. The film started ten minutes ago.
Shall we ..... come back tomorrow ..... ?

What about .... ?

3
go home
standing under the slide

c
Oh no! A stream! What shall we do?

Shall we .... ?

What about .... ?

(6) **Read and make your own suggestions. Use Shall we ... ? or What about ... ?**

1 You and your friend want to do something exciting.

....

2 It's raining and you and your friend are at your house.

....

3 An English girl is visiting you for the day.

....

Shall we meet in the park or at my house?

Writing Class: using *or* in questions

① **Look and write.**

1 Do you like ..../.......... ...tobogganing or skiing?...

2 Do you want to go ..../.......... .... ?

3 Shall we go ..../.......... .... ?

4 What about ..../.......... .... ?

② **Write suggestions.**

1 meet/in town/in the park? ...Do you want to meet in town or in the park?...

2 play tennis/football/in the morning? ....

3 have lunch/at my house/in a café? ....

4 go to the museum/the cinema/in the afternoon? ....

5 watch TV/play on the computer/in the evening? ....

③ **Write an email making suggestions for Saturday.**

Write:

- suggestions about where to meet.
- two suggestions about what to do in the morning.
- two suggestions about lunch.
- two suggestions about what to do in the afternoon.
- two suggestions about what to do in the evening.

Hi ....

I'm very happy that you are free on Saturday.

....

....

....

See you soon.

....

4 Number the dialogue in the correct order.

Tom

Amy

1 What shall we do this morning?

☐ What about surfing?

☐ OK. Let's go.

☐ Do you like rock climbing?

☐ I don't know. Have you got any ideas?

☐ I don't want to go surfing today.

☐ Yes, rock climbing is a great idea.

5 Choose and write.

want   know   ~~shall we~~   great idea   Do   What about

Amy: What **(1)** ....*shall we*................. do this afternoon, Tom?

Tom: I don't **(2)** .... Have you got any ideas?

Amy: **(3)** .... swimming?

Tom: I don't **(4)** .... to go swimming today.

Amy: **(5)** .... you like fishing?

Tom: Yes, fishing is a **(6)** ....

Amy: OK. Let's go.

6 Read the dialogues in Exercises 4 and 5 again and write.

1 Amy doesn't want to go .... in the morning.

2 She wants to go ....

3 Tom doesn't want to go .... in the afternoon.

4 He wants to go ....

FlyHigh File: Sporting legends

1 Match and write.

1	Olympic	medal	....
2	world	a goal	....
3	football	flag	Olympic flag
4	gold	player	....
5	score	record	....

2 Look and complete.

		Verb	Person
1		play tennis	tennis player
2		....	....
3		....	....
4		....	....
5		....	....

3 Circle the correct word.

1 How fast can you (run) / running?

2 He's an amazing tennis / tennis player.

3 I play football / football every weekend.

4 The team playing basket / play basketball really well.

5 Do you think she's a good swimmer / swimming.

(4) Read and write.

won   competed   records   ~~sportswoman~~   used   gold   Olympic   swimming

wheelchair

Tanni Grey-Thompson can't walk but she's an amazing
(1) sportswoman. She was born in Wales in 1969
and first **(2)** .... a wheelchair when she
was seven years old. She was good at sports and she
enjoyed **(3)** .... and horse riding. She
started wheelchair racing when she was thirteen and
six years later she **(4)** .... in the 1988 Seoul
Games. She's got eleven **(5)** .... medals,
which she **(6)** .... in five Paralympic
Games, the **(7)** .... Games for people who
can't walk or see well. She broke the world
(8) .... for 100 metres, 400 metres and
800 metres wheelchair racing. She also won the London
Wheelchair Marathon six times.

(5) Write True or False.

1 Tanni Grey-Thompson is from Wales. ....True........

2 She started using a wheelchair in 1979. ....

3 She was good at playing the drums. ....

4 She enjoyed cycling. ....

5 She competed in five Paralympic Games. ....

6 She's got eleven gold medals. ....

7 She won the New York Marathon six times. ....

(6) Read and complete the chart.

Sport	Tennis
Favourite player	
Nationality	
Age	
Titles and medals	

I like playing tennis. I like watching it too. There
are lots of great players but my favourite is Serena
Williams. She was born in America in 1981 and
started playing tennis when she was four years old.
Today she's one of the best tennis players in the
world and she's got 25 Grand Slam titles. She's also
got two Olympic gold medals. One day I want to be
a famous tennis player like Serena.

29 I'm going to phone the police!

1 Find and circle six items from a living room. Then write.

1 cushion
2 ....
3 ....
4 ....
5 ....
6 ....

c	u	r	t	a	i	n
u	w	u	y	i	k	o
s	v	g	b	s	e	r
h	a	c	l	a	m	p
i	s	x	u	z	a	j
o	e	m	w	e	e	a
n	s	o	f	a	g	t

2 Look, read and match.

2

1 He's throwing the ball.

2 She's phoning her friend.

3 She's going to phone her friend.

4 They're going to play football.

5 He's going to throw the ball.

6 They're playing football.

3 Match and circle.

1 There are lots of black clouds in the sky.

2 It's my mum's birthday tomorrow.

3 The sofa isn't comfortable.

4 My sisters are hungry.

5 My curtains are very old.

a They're going to have some stew / a shower.

b It's going to rain / snow.

c I'm going to buy some new ones / an old one.

d She's going to have a party / some water.

e We're going to get some more cushions / some more lamps.

④ Read, choose and write.

take   go   hide   ~~phone~~   catch

1 Look at that man and woman. They're dangerous thieves!

2 I ....'m going to phone.... the police.

3 The dog .... behind the tree.

4 He .... the money.

5 The police .... them!

6 They .... to prison!

⑤ Correct the sentences.

1 Mum and Dad going to watch TV.   Mum and Dad are going to watch TV.

2 I'm going look after my little brother. ....

3 We're going to playing a game. ....

4 He going to hide somewhere. ....

5 I'm going to looks for him. ....

6 It going to be fun. ....

30 Are they going to come home now?

① Read the clues and do the crossword.

1 You can wear this to a party.

2 It's a good idea to do this before you do something new.

3 To play or do things with your friends. (two words)

4 This is a long flag.

5 This is when you take food to eat outside.

6 You send these to your friends before a party.

② Write Is or Are and match.

1 ...Are............... they going to go on holiday?

2 .... he going to take his laptop with him?

3 .... we going to go to the airport?

4 .... she going to take some photos?

5 .... it going to rain?

6 .... you going to phone them?

a Yes, I am.

b No, he isn't.

c Yes, they are.

d No, it isn't.

e No, we aren't.

f Yes, she is.

(3) **Look and write questions and answers. Use going to.**

1 they/have/picnic ✔
2 they/take/photos ✘
3 the dog/swim/the river ✔
4 she/climb/a tree ✘
5 he/play/tennis ✘

1 Are they going to have a picnic?   Yes, they are.
2 ....
3 ....
4 ....
5 ....

(4) **Read and write.**

1 go/shops ✘   go/beach ✔   4 tidy/living room ✘   tidy/bedroom ✔
  She isn't going to go to the shops.   She ....
  She 's going to go to the beach.   She ....

2 make/cake ✘   make/invitations ✔   5 play/basketball ✘   play/football ✔
  I ....   We ....
  I ....   We ....

3 play/guitar ✘   play/drums ✔   6 paint/walls ✘   paint/banner ✔
  He ....   They ....
  He ....   They ....

(5) **What about you? Tick or cross. Then write true sentences.**

1 do my homework   ☐   4 have a dance lesson   ☐

2 have something to eat   ☐   5 tidy my bedroom   ☐

3 go for a swim   ☐   6 play on the computer   ☐

1 I'm going to do my homework after school./I'm not going to do my homework after school.
2 ....
3 ....
4 ....
5 ....
6 ....

31 Why did they want Toto?

1 Choose and write.

rare   robber   steal   jewellery   ~~valuable~~   paintings   Diamonds

1 A ...valuable... thing is usually very expensive.

2 .... are hard stones which usually have no colour.

3 You can see lots of famous .... in art galleries.

4 When something is ...., there aren't many of them in the world.

5 A .... is a person who takes something from someone without asking for it.

6 It's wrong to .... money.

7 You can wear .... around your neck, on your ears and on your fingers.

2 Circle and write. Use words from Exercise 1.

1 Claudia and Magnus are going to go to prison why / (because) they are ....

2 Why / Because did they .... Toto? Why / Because Claudia likes .... birds.

3 In their house in Switzerland the police found lots of ....

Why / because were they there?
Claudia and Magnus took them from art galleries why / because they are ....

4 There was lots of expensive ...., too.

Why / Because did Claudia steal it?
Why / Because she loves ....

3 Read and match.

1 Why are you going to the shops?   a Because I like swimming.

2 Why are you going to the bank?   b Because I want to read some books.

3 Why are you going to the pool?   c Because I've got a stomachache.

4 Why are you going to the library?   d Because I need some money.

5 Why are you going to the art gallery?   e Because I want to see some famous paintings.

6 Why aren't you eating your dinner?   f Because I want to buy some new clothes.

4 Read and write the correct letters.

a ~~Dr Wild, why are you an Animal Detective?~~
b Why did Claudia fall in the duck pond?
c Why did you go in the helicopter?
d Why did you take Jack and Kelly with you?

e Why did you call the police?
f Because Sally asked me to find Toto the toucan.
g Because he didn't drive carefully.
h Because we all love Oscar.

1 Reporter: ...a...
  Dr Wild: Because I love animals and I like finding them.

2 Reporter: Why did you go on this trip?
  Dr Wild: ....

3 Reporter: ....
  Dr Wild: Because they are helpful and friendly children.

4 Reporter: Why did your cat go with you?
  Dr Wild: ....

5 Reporter: ....
  Dr Wild: Because Claudia and Magnus were flying in one and we chased them.

6 Reporter: Why did Magnus crash into the tree?
  Dr Wild: ....

7 Reporter: ....
  Dr Wild: Because it was dark and she didn't see it.

8 Reporter: ....
  Dr Wild: Because Claudia and Magnus are dangerous robbers.

5 Choose and write.

my teachers are kind.
they are funny.
I can go to the beach.
I can play on my toboggan.

we learn interesting things.
we play games together.
~~it's warm and sunny~~.
there's lots of snow.

> I like summer because it's warm and sunny.

1 I like summer because _it's warm and sunny._
2 I like winter because ....
3 I like school because ....
4 I like friends because ....

32 Would you like to come to our party?

SKILLS

Writing Class: writing dates

① **Write the months in the correct order.**

June April ~~January~~ December May February October March July September August November

1 J anuary	**5** M	**9** S
2 F	**6** J	**10** O
3 M	**7** J	**11** N
4 A	**8** A	**12** D

② **Read and match.**

1 third	**a** 1st	**7** twenty-first	**g** 30th
2 first	**b** 2nd	**8** twenty-second	**h** 28th
3 fifth	**c** 3rd	**9** thirtieth	**i** 21st
4 second	**d** 4th	**10** thirty-first	**j** 22nd
5 sixth	**e** 5th	**11** twenty-eighth	**k** 20th
6 fourth	**f** 6th	**12** twentieth	**l** 31st

③ **Look and write the dates.**

a  **b**  **c** **d**

1 January 1st   **2** ....   **3** ....   **4** ....

④ **Write an invitation to a party.**

Write:
- what kind of party is it?
- where are you going to have it?
- what time is it going to be?
- what date are you going to have it?

PLEASE COME TO MY PARTY!

The occasion: ....

The time: ....

The date: ....

The place: ....

RSVP Tel: ....   Email: ....

⑤ Read and match.

1 Would you like   a Friday.
2 I'd   b to come to my party?
3 It's on   c is it?
4 What   d my house.
5 Where   e then!
6 It's at   f love to!
7 See you   g time is it?

⑥ Read Exercise 4 again and complete the dialogue.

(1) Would you like to come to my party?

Thank you. Yes, **(2)** ....! When is it?

(3) ....

(4) ....

It's at seven o'clock.

(5) ....

(6) ....

Bye

Great. **(7)** .... Bye.

⑦ Read and write.

Invitation

It's Mel's birthday on Saturday May 27th and she's going to have a picnic at five o'clock in the park.

a   b

Mel: Would you **(1)**

....?

Beth: Thank you, I'd love to! When **(2)**

.... ?

Mel: It's **(3)** ....

Beth: What time is it?

Mel: **(4)** ....

Beth: Where **(5)** .... ?

Mel: It's **(6)** ....

Beth: Great! See you then!

Mel: Bye!

FlyHigh File: Duke of Edinburgh's Award

① Choose and label the pictures.

Award   Physical   Volunteering   Expedition   ~~Skills~~

....

....

..... Skills .....

....

....

② Choose and write.

sports   help   ~~award~~   tent   fourteen   trip   animals   four   learn   photography

You can do The Duke of Edinburgh's **(1)** _award_ when you're **(2)** ....
or older. You have to do something from **(3)** .... sections. In the physical
section you play **(4)** .... or games. In the volunteering section you
(5) .... other people or **(6)** .... In the skills section you
(7) .... something new, like **(8)** .... or playing a musical
instrument and in the expedition section you go on a **(9)** .... with some
friends and sleep in a **(10)** .... for one night.

③ Read Exercise 2 again. Circle the correct answer.

1 You can do the awards when you're .... years old.

   a 12   **b** (14)   **c** 13

2 You can play football for the .... section.

   a physical   **b** volunteering   **c** skills

3 You can learn to play the guitar for the .... section.

   a physical   **b** volunteering   **c** skills

4 You sleep in a tent on the ....

   a award   **b** night   **c** expedition

④ Read and complete the chart below.

Hi, I'm Liam. I'm going to do the Bronze award. I'm going to help in an Old People's Home for the volunteering section because I know old people need a lot of help. I'm going to take photos for the skills section. I'm going to do that because I've got a new camera and I want to learn to take good photos.

I'm going to choose swimming for the physical section because I love swimming and I want to get better and faster. I'm going to go swimming three times a week and get a lifesaving award.

For the expedition, I'm going to ride my bike along the River Thames because I like riding my bike. Four of my friends and a teacher are going to come with me. We'll have to carry our tents and equipment on our bikes. I'm really looking forward to it!

	Volunteering	Skills	Physical	Expedition
What is Liam going to do?	Help in an Old People's Home.			
Why?				

⑤ Choose and complete the chart.

ride my bike to a farm   swim   help animals   write a story   walk up a mountain   paint
help children   play tennis

Hi, I'm Suzie. I'm going to ride my bike to a farm for the expedition.

Expedition	Volunteering	Physical	Skills
ride my bike to a farm	....	....	....
....	....	....	....

⑥ What about you? Complete.

For the expedition section I'd like to ....

For the volunteering section I'd like to ....

For the physical section I'd like to ....

For the skills section I'd like to ....

① **Match and write.**

diamond	lamp	painting	picnic	tools	compass
jewellery	knock over	**valuable**	have	borrow	lost
buy	chasing	**steal**	birthday	escape	use

1   The robber is going to ___steal___ the ___painting___ because it's ___valuable___ .

2   The woman is going to _____ the _____ because she likes _____ .

3   They're going to _____ the _____ because they're _____ .

4   The dog is going to _____ the _____ because it's _____ a cat.

5   The prisoner is going to _____ some _____ because he wants to _____ .

6   We're going to _____ a _____ because it's my _____ .

② **Choose and write. Use want to.**

eat a sandwich   open the window   drink some water   go to bed   ~~escape from prison~~

1   Claudia is unhappy. ___She wants to escape from prison.___

2   Magnus is hungry. _____

3   Dr Wild is hot. _____

4   Oscar is thirsty. _____

5   Jack and Kelly are tired. _____

4

③ **Read and circle the correct words.**

1 I like sports and I'm good at (running) / climb / play football.

2 He's happy when he's ice skate / skiing / toboggan.

3 My mum and dad like playing tennis / play volleyball / to surfing when we are on holiday.

4 Shall we to go fishing / go skateboard / go rock climbing this afternoon?

5 She wants jumping / to dive / swim in the swimming pool.

6 I've got a good idea. What about rollerblades / play basketball / cycling in the park?

④ **Choose and write.**

What about   Shall   Because   be   want to   going to
~~fancy dress~~   Why   pop star   costume

Ben: Look! It's a carnival. Look at all the **(1)** ..fancy dress... costumes.

Kate: **(2)** .... we join in?

Ben: Yes. I **(3)** .... be a superhero.

   What are you **(4)** .... wear?

Kate: I don't know.

Ben: **(5)** .... wearing this alien **(6)** .... ?

Kate: No, I'm going to **(7)** .... a pop star.

Ben: **(8)** .... do you want to be a **(9)** .... ?

Kate: **(10)** .... I like these silver shoes.

My English

How did I do? Write OK/Well/Very Well.

1 **Learn with Oscar**   She wants to swim/She likes swimming/She's good at diving/
   Shall we drive?/What about driving?/I'm going to walk ....

2 **New words**   alien/surfing/borrow/score/lamp/barrier/jewellery/silver .... banner

3 **Writing**   Email ....   Conversations ....

4 **Conversations**   Making suggestions ....   Making arrangements ....

5 **Projects**   Describing a sports person ....   Making a plan ....

The Voyages of Sindbad the Sailor

(1) Read and circle the correct word.

> **(1)** Sailors / Teachers work on **(2)** schools / ships at sea. The **(3)** captain / mother tells them what to do. They go away to sea for many weeks on long **(4)** cars / voyages. Sometimes the weather is bad and the sea is very **(5)** dangerous / sad. When it's stormy, the sailors are sometimes **(6)** afraid / happy of the sea. In the past ships were made of **(7)** colour / wood.

(2) Read **The Voyages of Sindbad the Sailor** on pages 100–101 of your Pupil's Book. Tick the correct picture.

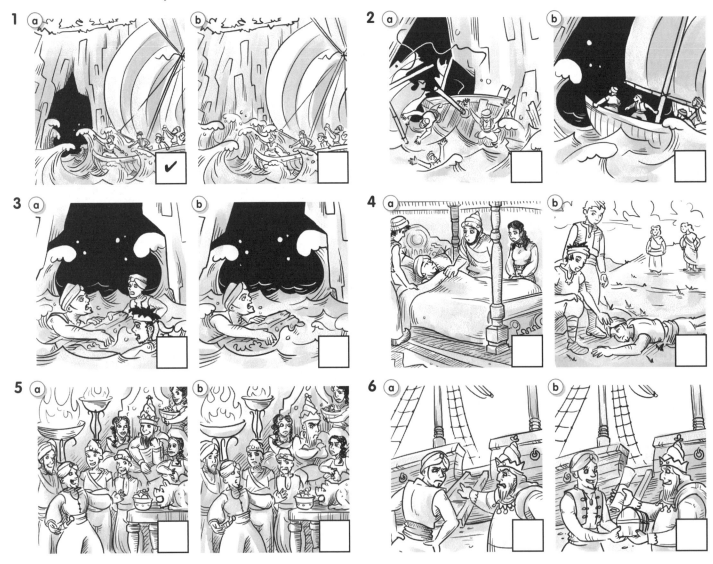

(3) Read and circle the correct words.

1 The captain ~~didn't want~~ / wanted to go into the cave.

2 Sindbad could / couldn't help the other sailors in the cave.

3 Sindbad woke up next to a river / a palace.

4 Sindbad knew the King of Serendip was dangerous / kind.

5 The King liked / didn't like Sindbad's stories.

6 Sindbad went / didn't go back to his home and his friends.

(4) Write True or False.

1 Sindbad wanted to go on lots more voyages.   False

2 Sindbad climbed the mountain.   ....

3 Sindbad went by train to the King of Serendip.   ....

4 The King of Serendip was a good man.   ....

5 Sindbad gave the King a letter.   ....

6 It was stormy when Sindbad went home.   ....

(5) Choose and write.

dangerous   stories   letter   afraid   ~~voyage~~   through   sailors   captain   ship

This was Sindbad's sixth **(1)** voyage .
The **(2)** .... saw a big mountain.
The weather was very bad and he couldn't stop the
(3) .... He was **(4)** ....
The ship went into a cave. It broke and the other
(5) .... couldn't swim in the
(6) .... sea. The water carried Sindbad
(7) .... the cave.

Sindbad woke up and saw lots of people. He went
to see the King of Serendip. The King was kind and
he liked listening to Sindbad's **(8)** ....
He gave Sindbad a **(9)** .... for his king
and many valuable things.

 **Jack has disappeared!**

① Choose and write.

~~return~~   hot air balloon   explain   disappear   trip

1	go or come back to a place	....return....
2	a visit somewhere for a few days	....
3	a form of transport that carries people up into the sky	....
4	make something clear	....
5	go where you can't be seen	....

② Match and write have or has.

1 He's worried because

2 I'm happy because

3 It's cold because

4 They're scared because

5 He's excited because

6 She's sad because

a they .... opened all the windows.

b his friends .... invited him to go on a trip to Wales.

c the bull .... escaped from the field.

d she .... dropped her doll in the river.

e the cat ....has.... disappeared again.

f I .... finished my homework.

③ Look and write.

1 ⓐ    ⓑ

Is the dog going to jump?

Yes, it ...'s jumped... in the river.

2 ⓐ    ⓑ

Is the cat going to knock over the cards?

Yes, it .... the cards and the pencils.

3 ⓐ    ⓑ

Is the fox going to disappear?

Yes, it .... behind the trees

4 ⓐ    ⓑ

Is the hot air balloon going to land?

Yes, it .... in the field.

4 Write and match.

1 We ...'ve tidied... (tidy) our   a France.
2 I .... (phone) my   b football boots.
3 She .... (return) to   c bedroom.
4 They .... (explain) the answers to the   d mum.
5 He .... (clean) his   e gate.
6 It .... (disappear) behind the   f homework.

5 Number and write.

4	turn on the radio He's turned on the radio.		drop a glass ....
	cook lunch		open the window ....
	return from a trip		wash and dry the dishes ....
	....		....

6 What about you? Tick the activities you have done today. Then write.

clean your teeth [✔]   dance [ ]   watch TV [ ]

walk to school [ ]   play a game [ ]   paint a picture [ ]

listen to music [ ]   phone a friend [ ]   use a computer [ ]

1   I've cleaned my teeth.   4 ....
2 ....   5 ....
3 ....   6 ....

34 Have you seen these photos?

① Look and number.

1 horse riding **2** Chinese **3** restaurant **4** ~~canoeing~~ **5** camping

 **4**

 ☐

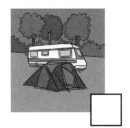 ☐

 ☐

 ☐

② Write. Use words from Exercise 1.

1 This is a place to eat.   _restaurant_

2 This word can be followed by *food, flag, girl, writing*.   ....

3 You can do these activities on holiday.   ....

③ Complete the chart.

Present	fly	....	....	sleep	send	be/go	....
Present perfect	have	have eaten	have ridden	have	have	have	have seen

④ Circle and write.

1 (Have) / Has you and your sister ever _flown_ (fly) in a helicopter?   No, we _haven't_ ....

2 Have / Has he ever .... (eat) in a Spanish restaurant?   Yes, he ....

3 Have / Has they ever .... (ride) on an elephant?   No, they ....

4 Have / Has the dog ever .... (sleep) on the sofa?   No, it ....

5 Have / Has she ever .... (see) a kangaroo?   Yes, she ....

6 Have / Has you ever .... (go) to an aquarium?   Yes, I ....

⑤ Look and write.

1 be   They <u>'ve been</u> to England.
             They <u>haven't been</u> to the USA.

2 fly   He _____ in a helicopter.
            He _____ in a plane.

3 sleep   She _____ in a tent.
            She _____ in a hotel.

4 see   They _____ an owl.
            They _____ a snake.

⑥ What about you? Write the questions and answer for you.

1 go/camping? <u>Have you ever been camping?</u>   Yes, I have./No, I haven't.

2 send/letter? _____ _____

3 climb/tree? _____ _____

4 go/horse riding? _____ _____

5 go/canoeing _____ _____

6 eat/Chinese? _____ _____

35 I haven't brushed Oscar yet!

1 Look and write the names.

a Rosie

b Millie

c Sonia

d Annie

e Lucy

f Jen

1 ....Millie.... 's brushing her hair.

2 .... 's brushing her teeth.

3 .... 's changing her clothes.

4 .... 's changing her book.

5 .... 's polishing her shoes.

6 .... 's polishing her jewellery.

2 Do the crossword. Write the past participles of the verbs.

1 change

2 give

3 paint

4 catch

5 go

6 fly

7 eat

8 open

9 have

4 c
h
a
6 n
g
8 e
d

③ Look, number and answer.

3	Has she painted a picture yet?	No, she hasn't.
	Has he caught a fish yet?	....
	Have they had their picnic yet?	....
	Has she opened the gate yet?	....
	Have they given the flowers to the woman yet?	....

④ Complete the sentences using yet.

1 The children have gone outside but Dr Wild hasn't gone outside yet .
2 Kelly has put her bag in the car but Jack ....
3 Dr Wild has seen her friends but the children ....
4 The children have looked at the photos but their friends ....

⑤ Correct the sentences.

1 I haven't looked at the newspapers yet. I haven't looked at the newspapers yet.
2 Have the police catched the thief yet? ....
3 Claudia and Magnus gone to prison. ....
4 Toto have flown around the garden. ....
5 Have they yet been to the zoo? ....
6 Dr Wild is given Toto back to the zoo. ....

⑥ Read, then write what Claire has and hasn't done.

Things to do	
brush teeth	✓
change clothes	✗
polish shoes	✓
wash hair	✓
pack bag	✗
give present to Anna	✗

1 She's brushed her teeth.
2 She hasn't changed her clothes yet.
3 ....
4 ....
5 ....
6 ....

36 SKILLS — You should take your camera.

Writing Class: writing an address

① Write the addresses in the correct order.

1
BS17 3DY   *Dr Sophie Wild*
8 Duke Street   ....
Dr Sophie Wild   ....
Bristol   ....

2
SW25 4QZ   *Mr M Wolf*
Tower Prison   ....
Mr M Wolf   ....
London   ....
Newgate Road   ....

② Write your address.

Name: ....

House number and street: ....

Town: ....

Postcode: ....

Country: ....

③ Write a postcard to a friend about your holiday.

Write:

- the address on the right, then write your message on the left.
- where you are and who you are with.
- about something you've seen.
- about something you've done.
- about something you want to do.

Dear ....
I've come to .... with
....
....
....
....
....
Love from ....

AIR MAIL POSTAL
30 C 493
JULY 2011

④ **Write sentences suggesting things to take on holiday. Use should.**

a camera   ~~a coat~~   an umbrella   your diary   some sun cream   a hat

1

> I think it will rain.

You _should take a coat._

You ....

2

> I think it will be hot.

You ....

You ....

3

> I think you will have a fantastic holiday.

You ....

You ....

⑤ **Choose and write.**

How long   good idea   first visit   ~~so excited~~   Five days   pretty country

Amy: I'm **(1)** _so excited_ . We're going to England tomorrow.

Max: Have you been there before?

Amy: No, I haven't It's my **(2)** ....

Max: **(3)** .... are you going for?

Amy: **(4)** ....

Max: It's a **(5)** .... You should take a video camera.

Amy: That's a **(6)** .... Thank you.

⑥ **Look at Exercise 5. Circle and answer the questions.**

1

Where's Amy going tomorrow?
She's going to _England._ ....

2

| April 3rd | May 15th | July 21st |
| Sept 3rd | June 19th | July 26th |

How long is she going for?

....

3

What's she going to take?

....

FlyHigh File: The Arctic and Antarctic

1 Circle and write the animals.

1 (seal)
2 light
3 scientist
4 walrus
5 ice
6 penguin
7 polar bear
8 dark
9 fox
10 temperature
11 whale
12 continent

.....seal.......... ....

2 Complete the sentences. Use the uncircled words in Exercise 1.

1 When water is very cold, it changes to ....ice...............

2 In winter the days are short and ....

3 When you are well your body .... is 37°C.

4 The Antarctic is a ....

5 In summer the days are long and ....

6 Marie Curie was a Polish .... who won two Nobel Prizes for science.

3 Read, choose and write.

winter   snow   reindeer   ~~Arctic~~   skiing   icy   Father Christmas   day   forests   never

My name's Aleksi and I come from Lapland in Finland. I live in Rovaniemi, a small town in the **(1)** ....Arctic........... Circle. It's famous because **(2)** .... lives here. In summer it is light all **(3)** .... In **(4)** .... it is always dark and the streets are very **(5)** .... but I like winter best because I love the **(6)** .... and I can go **(7)** .... When I'm skiing, I sometimes see wild animals. There are lots of birds and squirrels in the **(8)** .... Wolves and foxes also live there but you **(9)** .... see them. There are **(10)** .... too. Sometimes they come into the town.

4 Read and write the dates and names.

Date	The first person ...	Name
1820	The first person sees the Antarctic.	Captain Thaddeus Bellingshausen
	The first person reaches the South Pole.	
	The first person flies to the South Pole.	
	The first person born in the Antarctic.	

People have lived in the Arctic for thousands of years but we've known about the Antarctic for only two hundred years. The first person to see the Antarctic was a captain on a Russian ship, Thaddeus Bellingshausen, in 1820. There were many expeditions to the Antarctic in the nineteenth century but it was a difficult place to visit. Nobody reached the South Pole until the twentieth century. In 1911 a British expedition and an expedition from Norway raced each other to the South Pole. Roald Amundsen and his Norwegian team arrived on December 14th. A month later the British, led by Robert Scott, also reached the South Pole but the team died on the return journey. Eighteen years later Richard E Byrd, an American, flew to the South Pole and back. In 1978 the first child, an Argentinian called Emilio Marcos Palma, was born in the Antarctic. Even today the Antarctic has many visitors but nobody lives there all the time.

5 Read Exercise 4 again. Write True or False.

1 Nobody saw the Arctic before 1820.   ....

2 The first person to see the Antarctic was on a Russian boat.   ....

3 There weren't any expeditions to the Antarctic in the 19th century.   ....

4 The British and the Norwegians raced to the South Pole in 1911.   ....

5 The first person to fly to the South Pole was Argentinian.   ....

6 Thousands of people live in the Antarctic.   ....

The FlyHigh Review

1 Look and tick.

She's flown in a hot air balloon. ✔

She hasn't flown in a hot air balloon. ☐

The polar bear has caught a seal. ☐

The polar bear hasn't caught a seal. ☐

They've eaten Chinese food. ☐

They haven't eaten Chinese food. ☐

2 What about you? Complete and answer Yes, I have or No, I haven't.

1 eat/octopus. Have you ever eaten octopus? ....

2 see/penguin ....

3 polish/shoes ....

4 be/sailing ....

5 send/Valentine's Day card ....

6 score/goal ....

3 Write sentences using you should.

1 I eat sweets every day.
You should eat fruit every day.

4 I do my homework on the bus.
....

2 After school I play computer games.
....

5 I go to bed late.
....

3 I go to school by car every day.
....

6 I sleep six hours every night.
....

110

④ Look and answer the questions.

1 Are there many swans? — No, there aren't.

2 Is there a bridge across the river? ....

3 Do people live next to the lake? ....

4 Is the woman good at water skiing? ....

5 Is there anybody in the boat? ....

6 Is the boy wearing a hat? ....

7 Does the dog look friendly? ....

8 Can the girl swim? ....

⑤ What about you? Complete the sentences so they are true for you.

1 When I was three years old, I could ....

2 Last year I went ....

3 Every morning I have to ....

4 I'm happy when I ....

5 At the weekend I like ....

6 In the summer holidays I'm going to ....

My English

How did I do? Write OK/Well/Very Well.

1 Learn with Oscar It's disappeared/Have you ever seen a walrus/I haven't eaten yet ....

2 New words disappear/canoeing/polish/polar bear ....

3 Writing Postcard ....

4 Conversations Giving advice ....

5 Projects Making a chart about Australia ....

Pearson Education Limited
Edinburgh Gate
Harlow
Essex CM20 2JE
England
and Associated Companies throughout the world.

www.pearsonelt.com

© Pearson Education Limited 2011

The right of Jeanne Perrett and Charlotte Covill to be identified as authors of this Work has been asserted by them in accordance with the Copyright, Designs and Patents Act 1988.

All rights reserved; no part of this publication may be reproduced, stored in a retrieval system, or transmitted in any form or by any means, electronic, mechanical, photocopying, recording, or otherwise without the prior written permission of the Publishers.

First published 2011
Twelfth impression 2018

ISBN: 978-1-4082-4977-2

Printed in Malaysia, (CTP-VVP)

Set in VagRounded

Acknowledgements
The publisher would like to thank the following for their kind permission to reproduce their photographs:

(Key: b-bottom; c-centre; l-left; r-right; t-top)

Alamy Images: Colin Palmer Photography 44, Maurice Savage 46 (b); **Jon Barlow:** 82, 93b; **Trevor Clifford:** 9, 13, 83, 93t, 107; **Corbis:** Bettmann 109; **Fotolia.com:** Andreas Gradin 108b; **Getty Images:** Phil Cole 85, National Geographic / Mike Theiss 22 (d), US Coast Guard / Kyle Niemi 22 (c); **iStockphoto:** Steve Debenport 61b, fazon1 46 (d), Joshua Hodge Photography 108t; **NASA:** 71; **Pearson Education Ltd:** Gareth Boden 61t, Peter Evans 46 (c), Getty Images / Photodisc 22 (b), Imagestate / Michael Duerinckx 46 (a), Photodisc / StockTrek 22 (a); **Rex Features:** 46 (e)

All other images © Pearson Education

Every effort has been made to trace the copyright holders and we apologise in advance for any unintentional omissions. We would be pleased to insert the appropriate acknowledgement in any subsequent edition of this publication.

Illustrated by Diego Diaz/Lemonade Illustration; Sean Longcroft; Stephanie Strickland; Jurgen Ziewe/Debut Art; Dan Chernett/The Bright Agency